ISBN 978-1-331-76965-1
PIBN 10232411

This book is a reproduction of an important historical work. Forgotten Books uses
state-of-the-art technology to digitally reconstruct the work, preserving the original format
whilst repairing imperfections present in the aged copy. In rare cases, an imperfection in
the original, such as a blemish or missing page, may be replicated in our edition. We do,
however, repair the vast majority of imperfections successfully; any imperfections that
remain are intentionally left to preserve the state of such historical works.

Similar Books Are Available from
www.forgottenbooks.com

THE ABIDING PRESENCE
OF
THE HOLY GHOST IN THE SOUL

BY

THE VERY REVEREND
BEDE JARRETT, O.P.

THE CATHEDRAL LIBRARY ASSOCIATION
24-26 EAST 21ST STREET, NEW YORK
1918

PREFACE

In English-speaking countries the Church has been at a disadvantage in the way in which she has had to expound her doctrine, for she has been forced for many years to limit her attention just to those parts of her teaching wherein the Protestant bodies parted company from her. Without any desire to stir up barren controversy, she has naturally in self-defence been at pains most precisely to define those portions of her gospel most likely to be misunderstood. This has resulted, unfortunately, in her leaving in the background the other mysteries of faith, often richer in themselves, more helpful to her children. Now, however, that she is becoming more able to realize herself to the modern world, an opportunity opens for explaining hidden doctrines, of which the value to the Catholic in the development of his inner life is considerable.

It is to further this development that these meditations have been drawn up, since hardly anything can render us more sensible of our worth and Christian dignity than does the teaching of Our Lord on the indwelling of the Spirit of God. Cardinal Manning has indeed made this the subject of two volumes, *The Internal Working of the Holy Ghost* and *The Temporal Mission of the Holy Ghost*, which are still obtainable, and there are also such books as *Sermons on the Holy Ghost* (Cathedral Library Association).

But as yet in English there is no such direct exposition of Catholic teaching as Père Barthélemy Froget, O. P., has attempted in his *De l'Inhabitation du S. Esprit dans les ames justes* (Lethielleux, Paris, 1890). Like nearly all the doctrinal works of French origin, this treatise seems at times to suppose among the laity a deeper knowledge of the rudiments of scholastic philosophy than usually obtains among us, though the author has endeavored to help this out by occasional notes or explanations. To avoid this difficulty (which a mere translation would not lessen, but increase), the material of the book has been rearranged in a series of meditations which will, it is hoped, bring out in an easier form what might otherwise be too abstruse to be of general interest.

The wonderful beauty of the Church's teaching on this abiding presence of the Holy Ghost, while it deepens our acquaintance with His mysterious governance of the universe and discovers to us the hidden beauties of our soul's life, should bring also its measure of comfort, for whatever makes us conscious of the intimacy of God's dealing with us lessens life's greatest trouble, its loneliness.

BEDE JARRETT, O. P.

THE RECTORY OF
   OUR LADY OF LOURDES,

New York, February 11, 1918

TABLE OF CONTENTS

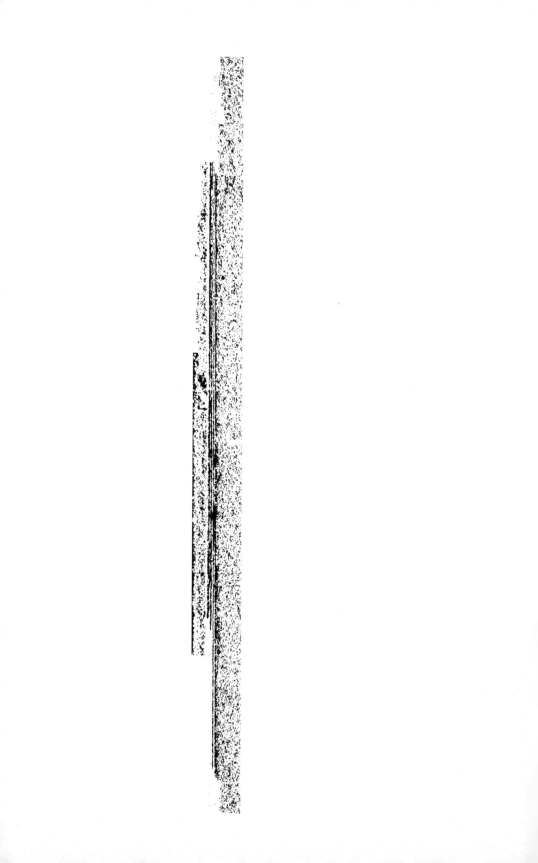

THE ABIDING PRESENCE OF THE HOLY GHOST IN THE SOUL

ENCYCLICAL LETTER FOR PENTECOST, 1897 [1]

To Our Venerable Brethren,
The Patriarchs, Primates, Archbishops,
Bishops, and Other Local Ordinaries
Having Peace and Communion with the
Holy See

LEO XIII, POPE

Venerable Brethren,
Health and Apostolic Benediction

That divine office which Jesus Christ received from His Father for the welfare of mankind, and most perfectly fulfilled, had for its final object to put men in possession of the eternal life of glory, and proximately during the course of ages to secure to them the life of divine grace, which is destined

[1] This translation is the official form that appeared in the London *Tablet*, June 5, 1897.

eventually to blossom into the life of heaven. Wherefore, our Saviour never ceases to invite, with infinite affection, all men, of every race and tongue, into the bosom of His Church: "Come ye all to Me," "I am the Life," "I am the Good Shepherd." Nevertheless, according to His inscrutable counsels, He did not will entirely to complete and finish this office Himself on earth, but as He had received it from the Father, so He transmitted it for its completion to the Holy Ghost. It is consoling to recall those assurauces which Christ gave to the body of His disciples a little before He left the earth: "It is expedient to you that I go: for if I go not, the Paraclete will not come to you: but if I go, I will send Him to you" (1 John 16.7). In these words He gave as the chief reason of His departure and His return to the Father, the advantage which would most certainly accrue to His followers from the coming of the Holy Ghost, and, at the same time, He made it clear that the Holy Ghost is equally sent by—and therefore proceeds from—Himself and the Father; that He would complete, in His office of Intercessor, Consoler, and Teacher, the work which Christ Himself had begun in His mortal life. For, in the redemption of the world, the completion of the work was by Divine Providence reserved to the manifold power of that Spirit who, in the creation, "adorned the heavens"

(Job 26.13), and "filled the whole world" (Wisdom 1.7).

THE TWO PRINCIPAL AIMS OF OUR PONTIFICATE

Now We have earnestly striven, by the help of His grace, to follow the example of Christ, Our Saviour, the Prince of Pastors, and the Bishop of our Souls, by diligently carrying on His office, entrusted by Him to the Apostles and chiefly to Peter, "whose dignity faileth not, even in his unworthy successor" (St. Leo the Great, Sermon 2, On the Anniversary of his Election). In pursuance of this object We have endeavored to direct all that We have attempted and persistently carried out during a long pontificate towards two chief ends: in the first place, towards the restoration, both in rulers and peoples, of the principles of the Christian life in civil and domestic society, since there is no true life for men except from Christ; and, secondly, to promote the reunion of those who have fallen away from the Catholic Church either by heresy or by schism, since it is most undoubtedly the will of Christ that all should be united in one flock under one Shepherd. But now that We are looking forward to the approach of the closing days of Our life, Our soul is deeply moved to dedicate to the Holy Ghost, who is the life-giving Love, all the work We have done during Our pontificate, that He may bring it to maturity and fruitfulness. In order the better and more fully to carry out this Our intention, We have resolved to address you at the approaching sacred season of Pentecost concerning the indwelling and miraculous power of the Holy Ghost; and the extent and efficiency of His action, both in the whole body of the Church and in the individual souls of its members, through the glorious abundance of His divine graces. We earnestly desire that, as a result, faith may be aroused in your minds concerning the mystery of the adorable Trinity, and especially that piety may increase and be inflamed towards the Holy Ghost, to whom especially all of us owe the grace of following the paths of truth and virtue; for, as St. Basil said, "Who denieth that the dispensations concerning man, which have been made by the great God and our Saviour, Jesus Christ, according to the goodness of God, have been fulfilled through the grace of the Spirit?" (Of the Holy Ghost, c. 16, v. 39.)

THE CATHOLIC DOCTRINE OF THE BLESSED TRINITY

Before we enter upon this subject, it will be both desirable and useful to say a few words about the Mystery of the Blessed

Trinity. This dogma is called by the doctors of the Church "the substance of the New Testament," that is to say, the greatest of all mysteries, since it is the fountain and origin of them all. In order to know and contemplate this mystery, the angels were created in Heaven and men upon earth. In order to teach more fully this mystery, which was but foreshadowed in the Old Testament, God Himself came down from the angels unto men: "No man hath seen God at any time; the only begotten Son, who is in the bosom of the Father, He hath declared Him" (John 1.18). Whosover then writes or speaks of the Trinity must keep before his eyes the prudent warning of the Angelic Doctor: "When we speak of the Trinity, we must do so with caution and modesty, for, as St. Augustine saith, nowhere else are more dangerous errors made, or is research more difficult, or discovery more fruitful" (*Summ. Th.* 1a, q. 31. *De Trin.* l. 1, c. 3). The danger that arises is lest the Divine Persons be confounded one with the other in faith or worship, or lest the one Nature in them be separated: for "This is the Catholic Faith, that we should adore one God in Trinity and Trinity in Unity." Therefore Our predecessor Innocent XII absolutely refused the petition of those who desired a special festival in honor of God the Father. For, although the separate mysteries connected with the Incarnate Word are celebrated on certain fixed days, yet there is no special feast on which the Word is honored according to His Divine Nature alone. And even the Feast of Pentecost was instituted in the earliest times, not simply to honor the Holy Ghost in Himself, but to commemorate His coming, or His external mission. And all this has been wisely ordained, lest from distinguishing the Persons men should be led to distinguish the Divine Essence. Moreover, the Church, in order to preserve in her children the purity of faith, instituted the Feast of the Most Holy Trinity, which John **XXII** afterwards extended to the Universal Church. He also permitted altars and churches to be dedicated to the Blessed Trinity, and, with the divine approval, sanctioned the Order for the Ransom of Captives, which is specially devoted to the Blessed Trinity and bears **Its** name. Many facts confirm this truth. The worship paid to the saints and angels, to the Mother of God, and to Christ Himself, finally redounds to the honor of the Blessed Trinity. In prayers addressed to one Person, there is also mention of the others; in the litanies after the individual Persons have been separately invoked, a common invocation of all is added: all psalms and hymns conclude with the doxology to the Father, Son, and Holy Ghost; blessings, sacred rites, and sacraments are either accompanied or concluded by the invocation of the Blessed Trinity. This was already foreshadowed by the Apostle in those words· "For of Him, and by Him, and in Him, are all things: to Him be glory for ever" (Rom. 11.36), thereby signifying both the Trinity of Persons and the Unity of Nature: for as this is one and the same in each of the Persons, so to each is equally owing supreme glory, as to one and the same God. St. Augustine, commenting upon this testimony, writes: "The words of the Apostle, *of Him, and by Him, and in Him,* are not to be taken indiscriminately; *of Him* refers to the Father, *by Him* to the Son, *in Him* to the Holy Ghost" (*De Trin.* l. vi, c. 10; l. i, c. 6). The Church is accustomed most fittingly to attribute to the Father those works of the Divinity in which power excels, to the Son those in which wisdom excels, and those in which love excels to the Holy Ghost. Not that all perfections and external operations are not common to the Divine Persons; for "the operations of the Trinity are indivisible, even as the essence of the Trinity is indivisible" (St. Aug. *De Trin.*, l. 1, cc. 4-5); because as the three Divine Persons "are inseparable, so do they act inseparably" (St. Aug., *ib*). But by a certain comparison, and a kind of affinity between the operations and the properties of the Persons, these operations are attributed or, as it is said, "appropriated" to One Person rather than to the others. "Just as we make use of the traces of similarity or likeness which we find in creatures for the manifestation of the Divine Persons, so do we use Their essential attributes; and this manifestation of the Persons by Their essential attributes is called *appropriation*" (St. Th. 1a, q. 39, xxxix, a. 7). In this manner the Father, who is "the principle of the whole God-head" (St. Aug., *De Trin.*, l. iv, c. 20), is also the efficient cause of all things, of the Incarnation of the Word, and the sanctification of souls; "of Him are all things": *of Him*, referring to the Father. But the Son, the Word, the Image of God, is also the exemplar cause, whence all creatures borrow their form and beauty, their order and harmony. He is for us the Way, the Truth, and the Life; the Reconciler of man with God. "By Him are all things": *by Him*, referring to the Son. The Holy Ghost is the ultimate cause of all things, since, as the will and all other things finally rest in their end, so He, who is the Divine Goodness and the Mutual Love of the Father and Son, completes and perfects, by His strong yet gentle power, the secret work of man's eternal salvation. "In Him are all things": *in Him*, referring to the Holy Ghost.

THE HOLY GHOST AND THE INCARNATION

Having thus paid due tribute of faith and worship owing to the Blessed Trinity, which ought to be more and more inculcated upon the Christian people, we now turn to the exposition of the power of the Holy Ghost. And, first of all, we must look to Christ, the Founder of the Church and the Redeemer of our race. Among the external operations of God, the highest of all is the mystery of the Incarnation of the Word, in which the splendor of the divine perfections shines forth so brightly that nothing more sublime can even be imagined, nothing else could have been more salutary to the human race. Now this work, although belonging to the whole Trinity, is still appropriated especially to the Holy Ghost, so that the Gospels thus speak of the Blessed Virgin: "She was found with child of the Holy Ghost," and "that which is conceived in her is of the Holy Ghost" (Matt. 1.18, 20). And this is rightly attributed to Him who is the love of the Father and the Son, since this "great mystery of piety" (1 Tim. 3.16) proceeds from the infinite love of God towards man, as St. John tells us: "God so loved the world as to give His only begotten Son" (John 3.16). Moreover, human nature was thereby elevated to a *personal* union with the Word; and this dignity is given, not on ac-

count of any merits, but entirely and absolutely through grace, and therefore, as it
were, through the special gift of the Holy
Ghost. On this point St. Augustine writes:
"This manner in which Christ was born of
the Holy Ghost, indicates to us the grace of
God, by which humanity, with no antecedent
merits, at the first moment of its existence,
was united with the Word of God, by so intimate a personal union, that He, who was
the Son of Man, was also the Son of God,
and He who was the Son of God was also
the Son of Man" (*Enchir.*, c. xl; St. Th.,
3a, q. xxxii, a. 1). By the operation of the
Holy Spirit, not only was the conception of
Christ accomplished, but also the sanctification of His soul, which, in Holy Scripture,
is called His "anointing" (Acts 10.38).
Wherefore all His actions were "performed
in the Holy Ghost" (St. Basil *de Sp. S.*, c.
xvi), and especially the sacrifice of Himself:
"Christ, through the Holy Ghost, offered
Himself without spot to God" (Heb. 9.14).
Considering this, no one can be surprised that
all the gifts of the Holy Ghost inundated the
soul of Christ. In Him resided the absolute
fullness of grace, in the greatest and most
efficacious manner possible; in Him were all
the treasures of wisdom and knowledge,
graces *gratis datae*, virtues, and all other
gifts foretold in the prophecies of Isaias
(Is. 4.1, 11.23), and also signified in that

miraculous dove which appeared at the Jordan, when Christ, by His baptism, consecrated its waters for a new sacrament. On this the words of St. Augustine may appropriately be quoted: "It would be absurd to say that Christ received the Holy Ghost when He was already thirty years of age, for He came to His baptism without sin, and therefore not without the Holy Ghost. At this time, then (that is, at His baptism), He was pleased to prefigure His Church, in which those especially who are baptized receive the Holy Ghost" (*De Trin.*, l. xv, c. 26). Therefore, by the conspicuous apparition of the Holy Ghost over Christ and by His invisible power in His soul, the twofold mission of the Spirit is foreshadowed, namely, His outward and visible mission in the Church, and His secret indwelling in the souls of the just.

The Holy Ghost and the Church

The Church which, already conceived, came forth from the side of the second Adam in His sleep on the Cross, first showed herself before the eyes of men on the great day of Pentecost. On that day the Holy Ghost began to manifest His gifts in the mystic body of Christ, by that miraculous outpouring already foreseen by the prophet Joel (2.28-29), for the Paraclete "sat upon the apostles as though new spiritual crowns were placed upon their heads in tongues of fire" (S. Cyril Hier. *Catech.* 17). Then the apostles "descended from the mountain," as St. John Chrysostom writes, "not bearing in their hands tables of stone like Moses, but carrying the Spirit in their mind, and pouring forth the treasure and the fountain of doctrines and graces" (*In Matt.* Hom. I, 2 Cor. 3.3). Thus was fully accomplished that last promise of Christ to His apostles of sending the Holy Ghost, who was to complete and, as it were, to seal the deposit of doctrine committed to them under His inspiration. "I have yet many things to say to you, but you cannot bear them now; but when He, the Spirit of Truth, shall come, He will teach you all truth" (John 16.12-13). For He who is the Spirit of Truth, inasmuch as He proceedeth both from the Father, who is the eternally True, and from the Son, who is the substantial Truth, receiveth from each both His essence and the fullness of all truth. This truth He communicates to His Church, guarding her by His all powerful help from ever falling into error, and aiding her to foster daily more and more the germs of divine doctrine and to make them fruitful for the welfare of the peoples. And since the welfare of the peoples, for which the Church was established, absolutely requires that this office should be continued for all time, the Holy Ghost perpetually supplies life and strength to preserve and increase the Church. "I will ask the Father, and He will give you another Paraclete, that He may abide with you for ever, the Spirit of Truth" (John 16.16, 17).

By Him the bishops are constituted, and by their ministry are multiplied not only the children, but also the fathers—that is to say, the priests—to rule and feed the Church by that Blood wherewith Christ has redeemed Her. "The Holy Ghost hath placed you bishops to rule the Church of God, which He hath purchased with His own Blood" (Acts 20.28). And both bishops and priests, by the miraculous gift of the Spirit, have the power of absolving sins, according to those words of Christ to the Apostles: "Receive ye the Holy Ghost; whose sins you shall forgive they are forgiven them, and whose sins you shall retain they are retained" (John 20.22, 23). That the Church is a divine institution is most clearly proved by the splendor and glory of those gifts with which she is adorned, and whose author and giver is the Holy Ghost. Let it suffice to state that, as Christ is the Head of the Church, so is the Holy Ghost her soul. "What the soul is in our body, that is the Holy Ghost in Christ's body, the Church" (St. Aug., *Serm.* 187, *de Temp.*). This being so, no further and fuller "manifestation **and** revelation of the Divine Spirit" may be imagined or expected; for that which now takes place in the Church is the most perfect possible, and will last until that day when the Church herself, having passed through her militant career, shall be taken up into the joy of the saints triumphing in heaven.

THE HOLY GHOST IN THE SOULS OF THE JUST

The manner and extent of the action of the Holy Ghost in individual souls is no less wonderful, although somewhat more difficult to understand, inasmuch as it is entirely invisible. This outpouring of the Spirit is so abundant, that Christ Himself, from whose gift it proceeds, compares it to an overflowing river, according to those words of St. John: "He that believeth in Me, as the Scripture saith, out of his midst shall flow rivers of living water"; to which testimony the Evangelist adds the explanation: "Now this He said of the Spirit which they should receive who believed in Him" (John 7.38, 39). It is indeed true that in those of the just who lived before Christ, the Holy Ghost resided by grace, as we read in the Scriptures concerning the prophets, Zachary, John the Baptist, Simeon, and Anna; so that on Pentecost the Holy Ghost did not communicate Himself in such a way "as then for the first time to begin to dwell in the saints, but by pouring Himself forth more abundantly; crowning, not beginning His gifts; not commencing a new work, but giving more abundantly" (St. Leo the Great, Hom. iii, *de Pentec.*).   But if they also were numbered among the children of God, they were in a state like that of servants, for "as long as the heir is a child he differeth nothing from a servant, but is under tutors and governors" (Gal. 4.1, 2).   Moreover, not only was their justice derived from the merits of Christ who was to come, but the communication of the Holy Ghost after Christ was much more abundant, just as the price surpasses in value the earnest and the reality excels the image.   Wherefore St. John declares: "As yet the Spirit was not given, because Jesus was not yet glorified" (John 7.39).   So soon, therefore, as Christ, "ascending on high," entered into possession of the glory of His Kingdom which He had won with so much labor, He munificently opened out the treasures of the Holy Ghost: "He gave gifts to men" (Eph. 4.8).   For "that giving or sending forth of the Holy Ghost after Christ's glorification was to be such as had never been before; not that there had been none before, but it had not been of the same kind" (St. Aug., *De Trin.*, l. iv, c. 20).

Human nature is by necessity the servant of God: "The creature is a servant; we are the servants of God by nature" (St. Cyr. Alex., *Thesaur.*, l. v, c. 5). On account, however, of original sin, our whole nature had fallen into such guilt and dishonor that we had become enemies of God. "We were by nature the children of wrath" (Eph. 2.3). There was no power which could raise us and deliver us from this ruin and eternal destruction. But God, the Creator of mankind and infinitely merciful, did this through His only begotten Son, by whose benefit it was brought about that man was restored to that rank and dignity whence he had fallen, and was adorned with still more abundant graces. No one can express the greatness of this work of divine grace in the souls of men. Wherefore, both in Holy Scripture and in the writings of the fathers, men are styled regenerated, new creatures, partakers of the Divine Nature, children of God, godlike, and similar epithets. Now these great blessings are justly attributed as especially belonging to the Holy Ghost. He is "the Spirit of adoption of sons, whereby we cry: Abba, Father." He fills our hearts with the sweetness of paternal love: "The Spirit Himself giveth testimony to our spirit that we are the sons of God" (Rom. 8.15, 16). This truth accords with the similitude observed by the Angelic Doctor between both operations of the Holy Ghost; for through Him "Christ was conceived in holiness to be by nature the Son of God," and "others are sanctified to be the sons of God by adoption" (St. Th. 3a, q. xxxii, a. 1). This spiritual generation proceeds from love in a much more noble manner than the natural: namely, from the uncreated Love.

The beginnings of this regeneration and renovation of man are by Baptism. In this sacrament, when the unclean spirit has been expelled from the soul, the Holy Ghost enters in and makes it like to Himself. "That which is born of the Spirit, is spirit" (John 3.6). The same Spirit gives Himself more abundantly in Confirmation, strengthening and confirming Christian life; from which proceeded the victory of the martyrs and the triumph of the virgins over temptations and corruptions. We have said that the Holy Ghost gives Himself: "the charity of God is poured out into our hearts by the Holy Ghost who is given to us" (Rom. 5.5). For He not only brings to us His divine gifts, but is the Author of them and is Himself the supreme Gift, who, proceeding from the mutual love of the Father and the Son, is justly believed to be and is called "Gift of God most High." To show the nature and efficacy of this gift it is well to recall the explanation given by the doctors of the Church of the words of Holy Scripture. They say that God is present and exists in all things, "by His power, in so far as all things are subject to His power; by His presence, inasmuch as all things are naked and open to His eyes; by His essence, inasmuch as He is present to all as the cause of their being" (St. Th. 1a, q. viii, a. 3). But God is in man, not only as in inanimate things, but because He is more fully known and loved by him, since even by nature we spontaneously love, desire, and seek after the good. Moreover, God by grace resides in the just soul as in a temple, in a most intimate and peculiar manner. From this proceeds that union of affection by which the soul adheres most closely to God, more so than the friend is united to his most loving and beloved friend, and enjoys God in all fullness and sweetness. Now this wonderful union, which is properly called "indwelling," differing only in degree or state from that with which God beatifies the saints in heaven, although it is most certainly produced by the presence of the whole Blessed Trinity— "We will come to Him and make our abode with Him" (John 14.23)—nevertheless is attributed in a peculiar manner to the Holy Ghost. For, whilst traces of divine power and wisdom appear even in the wicked man, charity, which, as it were, is the special mark of the Holy Ghost, is shared in only by the just. In harmony with this, the same Spirit is called Holy, for He, the first and supreme Love, moves souls and leads them to sanctity, which ultimately consists in the love of God. Wherefore the apostle, when calling us the temple of God, does not expressly mention the Father or the Son, but the Holy Ghost: "Know ye not that your members are the temple of the Holy Ghost, who is in you, whom you have from God?" (1 Cor. 6.19). The fullness of divine gifts is in many ways a consequence of the indwelling of the Holy Ghost in the souls of the just. For, as St. Thomas teaches, "when the Holy Ghost proceedeth as love, He proceedeth in the character of the first gift; whence St. Augustine saith that, through the gift which is the Holy Ghost, many other special gifts are distributed among the members of Christ" (*Summ. Th.*, 1a, q. xxxviii, a. 2. St. Aug., *de Trin.*, l. xv, c. 19). Among these gifts are those secret warnings and invitations, which from time to time are excited in our minds and hearts by the inspiration of the Holy Ghost. Without these there is no beginning of a good life, no progress, no arriving at eternal salvation. And since these words and admonitions are uttered in the soul in an exceedingly secret manner, they are sometimes aptly compared in Holy Writ to the breathing of a coming breeze, and the Angelic Doctor likens them to the movements of the heart which are wholly hidden in the living body. "Thy heart has a certain hidden power, and therefore the Holy Ghost, who invisibly vivifies. and unites the Church, is compared to the heart" (*Summ. Th.*, 3a, q. vii, a. 1, ad 3).   More than this, the just man, that is to say, he who lives the life of divine grace, and acts by the fitting virtues as by means of faculties, has need of those seven *gifts* which are properly attributed to the Holy Ghost.   By means of them the soul is furnished and strengthened so as to be able to obey more easily and promptly His voice and impulse.   Wherefore these gifts are of such efficacy that they lead the just man to the highest degree of sanctity; and of such excellence that they continue to exist even in heaven, though in a more perfect way.   By means of these gifts the soul is excited and encouraged to seek after and attain the evangelical beatitudes, which, like the flowers that come forth in the spring-time, are the signs and harbingers of eternal beatitude   Lastly, there are those blessed *fruits*, enumerated by the Apostle (Gal. 5.22), which the Spirit, even in this mortal life, produces and shows forth in the just; fruits filled with all sweetness and joy, inasmuch as they proceed from the Spirit, "who is in the Trinity the sweetness of both Father and Son, filling all creatures with infinite fullness and profusion" (St. Aug. *de Trin.*, l. vi, c. 9).   The Divine Spirit, proceeding from the Father and the Word in the eternal light of sanctity, Himself both Love and Gift, after having manifested Himself through the veils of figures in the Old Testament, poured forth all His fullness upon Christ and upon His mystic Body, the Church; and called back by His presence and grace men who were going away in wickedness and corruption with such salutary effect that, being no longer of the earth earthy, they relished and desired quite other things, becoming of heaven heavenly.

On Devotion to the Holy Ghost

These sublime truths, which so clearly show forth the infinite goodness of the Holy Ghost towards us, certainly demand that we should direct towards Him the highest homage of our love and devotion. Christians may do this most effectually if they will daily strive to know Him, to love Him, and to implore Him more earnestly; for which reason may this Our exhortation, flowing spontaneously from a paternal heart, reach their ears. Perchance there are still to be found among them, even nowadays, some who, if asked, as were those of old by St. Paul the Apostle, whether they have received the Holy Ghost, might answer in like manner: "We have not so much as heard whether there be a Holy Ghost" (Acts 19.2). At least there are certainly many who are very deficient in their knowledge of Him. They frequently use His name in their religious practices, but their faith is involved in much darkness. Wherefore all preachers and those having care of souls should remember that it is their duty to instruct their people more diligently and more fully about the Holy Ghost—avoiding, however, difficult and subtle controversies, and eschewing the dangerous folly of those who rashly endeavor to pry into divine mysteries. What should be chiefly dwelt upon and clearly explained is the multitude and greatness of the benefits which have been bestowed, and are constantly bestowed, upon us by this Divine Giver, so that errors and ignorance concerning matters of such moment may be entirely dispelled, as unworthy of "the children of light." We urge this, not only because it affects a mystery by which we are directly guided to eternal life, and which must therefore be firmly believed; but also because the more clearly and fully the good is known the more earnestly it is loved. Now we owe to the Holy Ghost, as we mentioned in the second place, love, because He is God: "Thou shalt love the Lord thy God with thy whole heart, and with thy whole soul, and with thy whole strength" (Deut. 6.5). He is also to be loved because He is the substantial, eternal, primal Love, and nothing is more lovable than love. And this all the more because He has overwhelmed us with the greatest benefits, which both testify to the benevolence of the Giver and claim the gratitude of the receiver. This love has a twofold and most conspicuous utility. In the first place, it will excite us to acquire daily a clearer knowledge about the Holy Ghost; for, as the Angelic Doctor says, "the lover is not content with the superficial knowledge of the beloved, but striveth to inquire intimately into all that appertains to the beloved, and thus to penetrate into the interior; as is said of the Holy Ghost, Who is the Love of God, that He searcheth even the profound things of God" (1 Cor. 2.10; *Summ. Theol.*, 1a, 2ae, q. 28, a. 2). In the second place, it will obtain for us a still more abundant supply of heavenly gifts; for whilst a narrow heart contracteth the hand of the giver, a grateful and mindful heart causeth it to expand. Yet we must strive that this love should be of such a nature as not to consist merely in dry speenlations or external observances, but rather to run forward towards action, and especially to fly from sin, which is in a more special manner offensive to the Holy Spirit. For whatever we are, that we are by the divine goodness; and this goodness is specially attributed to the Holy Ghost The sinner offends this his Benefactor, abusing His gifts; and taking advantage of His goodness becomes more hardened in sin day by day. Again, since He is the Spirit of Truth,

whosoever faileth by weakness or ignorance
may perhaps have some excuse before Al-
mighty God; but he who resists the truth
through malice and turns away from it, sins
most grievously against the Holy Ghost. In
our days this sin has become so frequent
that those dark times seem to have come
which were foretold by St. Paul, in which
men, blinded by the just judgment of God,
should take falsehood for truth, and should
believe in "the prince of this world," who is
a liar and the father thereof, as a teacher of
truth: "God shall send them the operation
of error, to believe lying (2 Thess. 2.10).
In the last times some shall depart from the
faith, giving heed to spirits of error and the
doctrines of devils" (1 Tim. 4.1). But
since the Holy Ghost, as We have said,
dwells in us as in His temple, We must repeat the warning of the Apostle: "Grieve
not the Holy Spirit of God, whereby you
are sealed" (Eph. 4.30). Nor is it enough
to fly from sin; every Christian ought to
shine with the splendor of virtue so as to be
pleasing to so great and so beneficent a
guest; and first of all with chastity and holiness, for chaste and holy things befit the
temple. Hence the words of the Apostle:
"Know you not that you are the temple of
God, and that the Spirit of God dwelleth
in you? But if any man violate the temple
of God, him shall God destroy. For the

temple of God is holy, which you are" (1 Cor. 3.16-17): a terrible, indeed, but a just warning.

Lastly, we ought to pray to and invoke the Holy Spirit, for each one of us greatly needs His protection and His help. The more a man is deficient in wisdom, weak in strength, borne down with trouble, prone to sin, so ought he the more to fly to Him who is the never-ceasing fount of light, strength, consolation, and holiness. And chiefly that first requisite of man, the forgiveness of sins, must be sought for from Him: "It is the special character of the Holy Ghost that He is the Gift of the Father and the Son. Now the remission of sins is given by the Holy Ghost as by the Gift of God" (*Summ. Th.*, 3a, q. iii, a. 8, ad 3m). Concerning this Spirit the words of the Liturgy are very explicit: "For He is the remission of all sins" (Roman Missal, Tuesday after Pentecost). How He should be invoked is clearly taught by the Church, who addresses Him in humble supplication, calling upon Him by the sweetest of names: "Come, Father of the poor! Come, Giver of gifts! Come, Light of our hearts! O, best of Consolers, sweet Guest of the soul, our refreshment!" (Hymn, *Veni Sancte Spiritus*). She earnestly implores Him to wash, heal, water our minds and hearts, and to give to us who trust in Him "the merit of virtue, the acquirement of salvation, and joy everlasting." Nor can it be in any way doubted that He will listen to such prayer, since we read the words written by His own inspiration: "The Spirit Himself asketh for us with unspeakable groanings" (Rom. 8.26). Lastly, we ought confidently and continually to beg of Him to illuminate us daily more and more with His light and inflame us with His charity: for, thus inspired with faith and love, we may press onward earnestly towards our eternal reward, since He "is the pledge of our inheritance" (Eph. 1.14).

Such, Venerable Brethren, are the teachings and exhortations which We have seen good to utter, in order to stimulate devotion to the Holy Ghost. We have no doubt that, chiefly by means of your zeal and earnestness, they will bear abundant fruit among Christian peoples. We Ourselves shall never in the future fail to labor towards so important an end; and it is even Our intention, in whatever ways may appear suitable, to further cultivate and extend this admirable work of piety. Meanwhile, as two years ago, in Our Letter *Provida Matris*, We recommended to Catholics special prayers at the Feast of Pentecost, for the Reunion of Christendom, so now We desire to make certain further decrees on the same subject.

An Annual Novena Decreed

Wherefore, We decree and command that throughout the whole Catholic Church, this year and in every subsequent year, a Novena shall take place before Whit-Sunday, in all parish churches, and also, if the local Ordinaries think fit, in other churches and oratories. To all who take part in this Novena and duly pray for Our intention, We shall grant for each day an Indulgence of seven years and seven quarantines; moreover, a Plenary Indulgence on any one of the days of the Novena, or on Whit-Sunday itself, or on any day during the Octave; provided they shall have received the Sacraments of Penance and the Holy Eucharist, and devoutly prayed for Our intention. We will that those who are legitimately prevented from attending the Novena, or who are in places where the devotions cannot, in the judgment of the Ordinary, be conveniently carried out in church, shall equally enjoy the same benefits, provided they make the Novena privately and observe the other conditions. Moreover, We are pleased to grant, in perpetuity, from the Treasury of the Church, that whosoever, daily, during the Octave of Pentecost up to Trinity Sunday inclusive, offer again publicly or privately any prayers, according to their devotion, to the Holy

Ghost, and satisfy the above conditions, shall a second time gain each of the same Indulgences. All these Indulgences We also permit to be applied to the suffrage of the souls in Purgatory.

And now Our mind and heart turn back to those hopes with which We began, and for the accomplishment of which We earnestly pray, and will continue to pray, to the Holy Ghost. Unite, then, Venerable Brethren, your prayers with Ours, and at your exhortation let all Christian peoples add their prayers also, invoking the powerful and ever-acceptable intercession of the Blessed Virgin. You know well the intimate and wonderful relations existing between her and the Holy Ghost, so that she is justly called His Spouse. The intercession of the Blessed Virgin was of great avail both in the mystery·of the Incarnation and in the coming of the Holy Ghost upon the Apostles. May she continue to strengthen our prayers with her suffrages, that, in the midst of all the stress and trouble of the nations, those divine prodigies may be happily revived by the Holy Ghost, which were foretold in the words of David: "Send forth Thy Spirit and they shall be created, and Thou shalt renew the face of the earth" (Ps. 103.30).

As a pledge of Divine favor and a testimony of Our affection, Venerable Brethren, to you, to your Clergy and people, We gladly impart in the Lord the Apostolic Benediction.

Given at St. Peter's, in Rome, on the **9th** day of May, **1897**, in the **20th** year of **Our** Pontificate.

LEO XIII, POPE.

God's Presence

1. Scripture is very full of the idea of the nearness of God to His creation, the Old Testament is alive with that inspiration, for there is hardly a chapter or verse that does not insist upon that truth. Naturally the New Testament, teaching so tenderly the Fatherhood of God, is even more explicit and more beautiful in its references to this intimate relationship. To the Athenians, St. Paul can develop no other point than this, and he finds in moving accents an eloquent appeal voiced by the touching dedication of an altar to the *Unknown God.* Now this notion of God's nearness to His world depends for its full appreciation on the central doctrine of creation. He has made the world, in consequence it is impressed with His personality; the more vigorous the artificer—the more vigorous that he is in character, will and personality, the more is his work stamped with his individuality; hence, the tremendous personality of God must be everywhere traceable in the things He has made.

2. When we say God is everywhere, we mean that He is in all things because He made all things. Not only does the whole

world lie outstretched before His eye and is
governed by His power, but He Himself
lurks at the heart of everything. By Him
things have come into existence, and so
wholly is that existence of theirs His gift,
that were He to withdraw His support they
would sink back into nothingness. It is a perpetual remark about man's works that they
outlast him. Organizations we have toiled
to establish outgrow our fostering care, perhaps grow tired of our interference and long
to be free of our regulations. Wordsworth
tells how a monk in Spain, pointing to the
pictures on the walls of the monastery, which
remained while the generations looking at
them passed away, judged: "We are the
shadows, they the substance." But the relationship established by creation is of a far
greater dependence, so that nothing God has
made can exist without His support. Out of
human acts it is only music that bears some
resemblance to this, for when the voice is
silent there is no longer any song.

3. God, then, is within all creation, because He is its cause. He is within every
stone and leaf and child. Nothing, with life
or without, evil or good, can fail to contain
Him as the source of its energy, its power,
its existence; He is "the soul's soul." Not
only, therefore, must I train myself to see
with reverence that everything contains Him,
but I must especially realize His intimacy

and relationship to myself.   Religion, indeed,
in practice is little else than my personal
expression of that relationship.   I have in
my prayers, in my troubles, in my temptations, to turn to God, not without but within,
not to some one above me or beneath supporting me, but right at the core of my
being.   I can trace up to its source every
power of my soul, my intelligence, my will,
my love, my anger, my fear, and I shall find
Him there.   Nothing but opens its doors to
Him as innermost in its shrine.   Wholly is
God everywhere, not as some immense being
that with its hugeness fills the world, but as
something that is within every creature He
has made.

DEGREES OF GOD'S PRESENCE

1. God is intimate with all creation because He made it, for creation implies that God remains within, supporting, upholding. God is within everything, and therefore He is everywhere. But while we thus believe that God is wholly everywhere, we also believe something which seems the exact opposite, for we believe that God is more in some places than in others, more in some people than in others. How is it if God is wholly everywhere that He can be more here than there? To understand this we must also understand that every created thing shares somehow in God's being. He communicates Himself to it in some fashion, for apart from Him it could have no perfections. We have a way of saying that we reflect God's greatness and that we are "broken lights" of Him. But that is far short of the truth; we do more than reflect, we actually have some participation in God, so that St. Thomas boldly takes over a saying of Plato: "The individual nature of a thing consists in the way it participates in the perfections of God" (*Summa* 1, 14.6). Not, of course, that there is any community of being, but a direct participation.

2. Now since everything participates in God and since some things are more excellent than others, it stands to reason that some things express God better than others. The eyes of a dog often are pitiful to see, because we can note its evident desire and yet its impossibility to express its feelings. The whole of nature has to seeing minds the same pitifulness. It is always endeavoring to express God, the inexpressible. Yet the higher a thing is in the scale of being the more of God it expresses, for it participates more in God's being. The more life a thing has and the more freedom it acquires, then the nearer does it approach to God and the more divinity it holds. Man, by his intelligence, his deeper and richer life, his finer freedom, stands at the head of visible creation, and, in consequence, is more fully a shrine of God than lower forms of life. He bears a closer resemblance to the Divine intelligence and will and has a greater share in them. It is then in that sense that we arrange in ascending order inanimate creation, the vegetable kingdom, the animal kingdom, and man.

3. Consequently we can now see in what sense God is said to be more in one thing than in another. He is more in it because He exercises Himself more in one thing than in another; one thing expresses more than another the perfections of God because it shares

more deeply than another that inner being of God. The more nearly anything or any one is united to God the more does His power exercise itself in them, so that, since God's gifts are variously distributed and are of various degrees, we are justified in saying that though He is wholly everywhere, He may be more fully here than there, just as, though my soul is in every part of my being, it is more perfectly in the brain than elsewhere, because there it exercises itself more fully and with more evidence of expression. Thus we say God is more in a man's soul than anywhere else in creation, since in a man's soul God is more perfectly expressed. It is therefore with great reverence that I should regard all creation, but with especial reverence that I should look to the dignity of every human soul.

God's Special Presence in the Just

1. While God is in everything in creation, He dwells in the just by grace. Scripture quite noticeably uses the word *dwelling* when it wishes to express the particular way in which God is present in the souls of the just. He is in all things; in the just He dwells. The same word actually is applied to the presence of God in the souls of those in grace as is used when speaking of God's presence in the Temple. But here again it is necessary to say that God's dwelling in the Temple never implied He was not elsewhere, but did imply that somehow His presence in the Temple was quite different from the way in which He was present elsewhere. Just then the same kind of difference between the presence of God in all created nature and His presence in the souls of the just is intended by the careful use in Scripture of the word dwelling, viz., that God has, over and above His ordinary presence in every single created thing, a further and especial presence in the hearts of those in friendship with Him by grace, and this new presence is a fuller and richer presence whereby God's excellencies and perfections are more openly displayed.

2. Another way in which the same idea is pressed home in the New Testament is by the word *sent* or *given*. Frequently, in the last discourse of Our Lord on the night before He suffered, He spoke to the Apostles of the Holy Spirit, the Paraclete, the Comforter who was to be sent or given. Now, ordinarily, by using the expression, "sending some one," we imply that now the person sent is where he was not before, that he has passed from here to there. Obviously Our Lord cannot really mean that only after His crucifixion and ascension would the Holy Ghost be found in the hearts of the Apostles, for we have already insisted that in every creature there must be, by virtue of its very creation, the Holy Spirit at the heart of it. Hence the only possible meaning is that the Holy Spirit will descend upon the Apostles and become present within them after some new fashion in which He was not before. "Because you are His children God has sent into your hearts the spirit of His Son whereby you cry Abba: Father" (Gal. 4.6). From the beginning the Holy Ghost had been within them; now His presence there is new and productive of new effects.

3. By God's indwelling, then, effected by grace, the Holy Spirit now is present in the soul differently from the way in which He is present by creation. By creation He is wholly everywhere, yet more in the higher forms than in the lower, for He is able to express more of Himself in them. Among these highest forms of visible creation, namely, man, there are again degrees of His presence, so that even among men He is more in one than in another. This gradation is in proportion to their grace. The more holy and sanctified they become, the more does the Holy Spirit dwell in them, the more fully is He sent, the more completely given, while the Book of Wisdom says expressly that God does not dwell in sinners. As soon as I am in a state of grace the Holy Ghost dwells in me in this new and wonderful way, takes up His presence in me in this new fashion. It is precisely, then, by our faith and hope and love that this is effected, so that the individual soul under God's own movement does help on this union of God and man. In all the rest of creation God is present by His action; in the souls of the just it is true to say that He is present by theirs.

NATURE OF THIS PRESENCE

1. We have taken it for granted that God then is present somehow in the soul by grace. We have now to consider what sort of a presence this really is. Do we mean absolutely that God the Holy Ghost, is truly in the soul Himself, or do we, by some metaphor or vague expression, mean that He is merely exerting Himself there in some new and especial way? Perhaps it is only that by means of the sevenfold gifts He has got a tighter hold of us and can bring us more completely under the sweet dominion of His will. All that is true, but all that is not enough, for we do absolutely mean what we say when we declare that by grace the Holy Spirit of God is present within the soul. Scripture is exceedingly full of the truth of this and is always insisting on this presence of the Holy Ghost. St. Paul, especially, notes it over and over again, and in his epistle to the Romans repeats it in very forcible language: "But you are not in the flesh but in the spirit, if so be that the spirit of God dwell in you" (Romans 8.9), and he goes on in that same chapter to imply that this presence is a part of grace.

2. To some it will seem curious to find

that the Fathers of the Church in earliest
ages were not only convinced of the fact of
this presence, but appealed triumphantly to
it as accepted even by heretics. When, in
the early days, a long controversy raged as to
whether the Holy Ghost was really God or
not, the Fathers argued that since this indwelling of the Spirit was acknowledged on
all hands, and since it was proper to God
only to dwell in the heart of man, the only
possible conclusion was that the Holy Ghost
was Divine. The value of the argument is
not here in question, but it is interesting to
find that this presence was so generally believed in as part of the Christian Faith. In
the acts of the martyrs, too, there are frequent references to this, as when St. Lucy
declared to the judge that the Spirit of God
dwelt in her, and that her body was in very
truth the temple and shrine of God. Again,
Eusebius relates in his history that Leonidas,
the father of Origen, used to kneel by the
bedside of the sleeping boy and devoutly and
reverently kiss his breast as the tabernacle
wherein God dwelt. The child in his innocence and grace is indeed the fittest home on
earth for God.

3. This presence, then, of God in the soul
is a real, true presence, as real and as true
as the presence of Our Lord Himself in the
Blessed Sacrament of the Eucharist. We
look on all that mystery as very wonderful,

and indeed it is, that day by day we can be made one with God the Son by receiving His Body and Blood; we know the value to be got out of visits to His hidden presence, the quiet and calm peace such visits produce in our souls; yet so long as we are in a state of grace the same holds true of the Holy Spirit within us. We are not indeed made one with the Holy Ghost in a substantial union such as united together in the Sacred Incarnation God and man; nor is there any overpowering of our personality so that it is swamped by a Divine Person, but we retain it absolutely. The simplest comparison is our union with Our Lord in the Holy Eucharist, wherein we receive Him really and truly and are made partakers of His divinity. By grace, then, we receive really and truly God the Holy Ghost and are made partakers of His divinity. If, then, we genuflect to the tabernacle in which the Blessed Sacrament is reserved and treat our Communions as the most solemn moments of our day, then equally we must hold in reverence every simple soul in a state of grace, the souls of others and our own.

THE MODE OF THIS PRESENCE: OBJECT OF KNOWLEDGE

1. The fact, then, of this presence has been established and its nature explained. It is a real presence, a real union between the soul and God the Holy Ghost. We have, however, a further point to elucidate, the mode whereby this presence is effected. Now this is twofold in so far as this presence of the Spirit affects the mind and heart of man. First, then, we take the knowledge of God that by this presence is generated in the soul. By natural knowledge we can argue not only to the existence of God, but in some way also to His nature. Not only do we know from the world which He has made that He certainly must Himself have a true existence, but we can even, gradually and carefully, though certainly with some vagueness, argue to God's own divine attributes. His intelligence is evident, His power, His wisdom, His beauty, His providence, His care for created nature. The pagans merely from the world about them painfully, and after many years and with much admixture of error, could yet in the end have their beautiful thoughts about God, and by some amazing instinct have stumbled upon truths

which Christianity came fully to establish. The writings of Plato and Aristotle, of some Eastern teachers, of some of the Kings and priests of Egypt, are evidences of the possibility of the natural knowledge about God.

2. Faith, then, came as something over and above the possibilities of nature, not merely as regards the contents, but also as regards the kind of knowledge. Reason argues to God, and, therefore, attains God indirectly. It is like getting an application by letter from an unknown person and guessing his character from the handwriting, the paper, the ink, the spelling, the style. Possibly by this means a very fair estimate may be formed of his capacities and his fitness for the position which we desire him to fill. But faith implies a direct contact with the person who has written the letter. Before us is spread what Longfellow has called "the manuscript of God," and from it we argue to God's character. Then faith comes and puts us straight into connection with God Himself. Theological virtues are the names given to faith, hope, and charity, because they all have God for their direct and proper object. Faith then attains to the very substance of God. It is indeed inadequate in so far as all human forms of thought can only falteringly represent God as compared with the fullness that shall be revealed hereafter, still for all that it gives us, not indirect but

direct knowledge of Him. I do not argue by faith to what God is like from seeing His handiwork; but I know what He is like from His descriptions of Himself.

3. Now the indwelling of the Spirit of God gives us a knowledge of God even more wonderful than faith gives, for even faith has to be content with God's descriptions of Himself. In faith I am indeed listening to a Person Who is telling me all about Himself. He is the very truth and all He says is commended to me by the most solemn and certain of motives; but I am still very far from coming absolutely into direct and absolute experience of God. That, indeed, fully and absolutely, can be achieved only in Heaven. It is only there in the beatific vision that the veils will be wholly torn aside and there will be a face to face sight of God, no longer by means of created, and therefore limited, ideas, but an absolute possession of God Himself. Yet though absolutely I must wait for Heaven before I can achieve this, it is none the less true that I can begin it on earth by means of this indwelling of the Spirit of God. This real presence of God in my soul can secure for me what is called an experimental knowledge of God, such as undoubtedly I do have. It is not only that I believe, but I know. Not only have I been told about God, but, at least, in passing glimpses, I have seen Him. We may almost

say to the Church what the men of Sichar said to the woman of Samaria, "We now believe, not for thy saying, for we ourselves have heard and know" (John 4.42). "For the Spirit Himself giveth testimony to our spirit that we are the sons of God" (Romans 8.16).

MODE OF THIS PRESENCE: OBJECT OF LOVE

1. There is something that unites us more closely to our friends than knowledge does, and this is love. Knowledge may teach us about them, may unlock for us gradually throughout life ever more wonderful secrets of their goodness and strength and loyalty. But knowledge of itself pushes us irresistibly on to something more. The more we know of that which is worth knowing, the more we must love it. Now love is greater than knowledge whenever knowledge itself does not really unite us to the object of our knowledge, so that St. Paul can deliberately put charity above faith, since faith is the knowledge of God by means of ideas which are themselves created and limited and inadequate, while charity sweeps us up and carries us right along to God Himself. Hence it was an axiom among the mediæval theologians that love is more unifying than knowledge, so that in the real indwelling of the Holy Spirit in our hearts we must expect to find not only that He is the object of our intelligence, but also that He has a place in our hearts. Indeed, it is impossible to conceive any experimental knowledge which does not also include in it the notion of love.

2. This love or friendship between ourselves and the Holy Spirit, if by friendship we mean anything like that of which we have experience in our human relations, implies three things. First of all, friendship implies that we do not love people for what we can get out of them, for that would be an insult to a friend, for it would mean selfishness or even animal passion. Friendship implies that we come for what we can give far more than that we come for what we can get. We love because we have helped is more often the true order of the origins of friendship than we help because we have loved. Secondly, friendship to be complete must be mutual. There may indeed be love when some poor, forlorn soul is here never requited in its affection, but that is not what we mean by a friend or by friendship. Friendship implies action, a fellow feeling, a desire for each other, a sympathy. Thirdly, friendship also implies necessarily a common bond of likeness, or similarity of condition or life, some equality. Of course it is evident from classic instances that friendship may exist between a shepherd lad and the son of a king (though perhaps Jonathan's princedom was very little removed from shepherd life), yet the very friendship itself must produce equality between them. Said the Latin proverb: "Friendship either finds, or makes men equal."

3. Now, therefore, to be perfectly literal in our use of the word, we must expect to find these things reproduced in our friendship with the Spirit of God; and, wonderful as it is, these things are reproduced. For God certainly loves us for no benefit that He can obtain from His love. He certainly had no need of us, nor do we in any sense fill up anything that is wanting to His life. Before we were, or the world was created, the Ever Blessed Three in One enjoyed to the full the complete peace and joy and energy of existence. We are no late development of His being, but only came because of His inherent goodness that was always prodigal of itself. He is our friend, not for His need, but for ours. He is our friend, not for what He could get, but for what He could give—His life. Again, His friendship is certainly mutual, for as St. John tells: "Let us therefore love God because God first hath loved us" (John 4.19). There is no yearning on our part which is not more than paralleled on His. I can say not only that I love God, but that He is my friend. Thirdly, I may even dare to assert that there is a common bond of likeness and equality between myself and Him. He has stooped to my level only that He may lift me to His own. He became Man that He might make man God, and so, equally, the Holy Spirit dwells in me that I may dwell in Him. "Friendship either

finds, or makes men equal." It found us apart, it makes us one. He came divine, perfect, to me human, imperfect. By grace I am raised to a supernatural level. I know Him in some sort as He is; I am immediately united to Him by the bond of love.

This Presence is of the Same Nature as that in Heaven

1. This union, then, between God and my soul, effected by grace, is real and true. It is something more than faith can secure, a nearer relationship, a deeper, more personal knowledge, a more ardent and personal love. Indeed, so wonderful is the union effected that the teaching of the Church has been forcibly expressed in Pope Leo XIII's *Encyclical*, by saying that the only difference between it and the Vision of Heaven is a difference of condition or state, a difference purely accidental, not essential. Heaven, with all its meaning, its wonders of which eye and ear and heart are ignorant, can be begun here. Moreover, it must be insisted upon, that this is not merely given to chosen souls whose sanctity is so heroic as to qualify them for canonization; it is the heritage of every soul in a state of grace. When I step outside the confessional box after due repentance and the absolution of the priest, I am in a state of grace. At once, then, this blessed union takes effect. Within me is the Holy Spirit, dwelling there, sent, given. As the object of knowledge He can be experienced by me in a personal and familiar way.

I can know Him even as I am known. As the object of love He becomes my friend, stooping to my level, lifting me to His. At once, then, though still in a merely rudimentary way, can dawn upon me the glories of my ultimate reward. Even already, upon earth, I have crossed the threshold of Heaven.

2. In order for me to enjoy that ultimate vision of God, two things will be necessary for me. First, I shall need to be strengthened so as to survive the splendor and joy of it. No man can see God and live, for like St. Paul on the road to Damascus, the splendor of the vision would wholly obscure the sight. Just as a tremendous noise will strain the hearing of the ear, or an overbright light will dazzle the eyes to blindness, or an overwhelming joy will break the heart with happiness, so would the vision of God strike with annihilation the poor weak soul. Hence the light of glory, as it is called by the theologians, has to be brought into use. By this is meant that strengthening of the human faculties which enables them without harm to confront the Truth, Goodness, Power, Beauty of God. Secondly, this vision implies an immediate contact with God. It is no question simply of faith or hope, but of sight and possession, so that there should be no more veils, no more reproductions or reflections of God, but God Himself. Those two things sum up what we mean by the Beatific Vision.

Now, then, if there is a similarity of kind between that union in heaven and the union that can be reflected on earth, then grace in this life must play the part of the light of glory in the next, and I must be able in consequence to enter into personal relations and immediate contact with God.

3. Such, then, is the likeness between the indwelling of the Spirit on earth, and the beatific vision. Wherein comes the difference? The difference one may say is largely a difference of consciousness. Here on earth I have so much to distract me that I cannot possibly devote myself in the same way as then I shall be able to do. There are things here that have got to be done, and there is the body itself which can only stand a certain amount of concentration and intensity. If strained too much it just breaks down and fails. All this complicates and hampers me. But in heaven I shall take on something (of course a great' deal intensified) of the consciousness and alertness of youth. A child can thoroughly enjoy itself, for it has got the happy faculty of forgetting the rest of life, all its troubles, anxieties, fears. Heaven, then, means the lopping off of all those menaces, and the consequent full appreciation of God in knowledge and love. Hence I must not be disturbed if here on earth all these wonderful things which I learn about concerning the indwelling of the Holy Spirit do not seem

to take place. It is very unfortunate that I do not appreciate them, but it is something at least to know that they are there. It is a nuisance that I do not see Him, but it is something at least to be certain He is within me.

This Presence Common to the Whole Trinity

1. So far it has been taken for granted that this indwelling is proper to the Holy Spirit, but it must now be added that indeed it is really an indwelling of the Blessed Trinity. It is true that very seldom does Scripture speak of the Three Persons as dwelling in the soul, still less of Their being given or sent. But every reason for which we attribute this to the Holy Ghost would ·hold equally well of the other Two Persons. By grace we are made partakers of God's Divine nature; He comes to us as the object of our knowledge and our love. Why should we suppose that this Divine Presence applies directly only to the Spirit of God? The only reason, of course, is the impressive wording of the New Testament. But even here there are equally strong indications that more than the Holy Ghost is implied: "If any man will love Me he will keep My word, and My Father will love him, and We will come to him, and will make Our abode with him. . . . But the Paraclete, the Holy Ghost, whom the Father will send in My name, He will teach you all things and bring all things to your mind whatsoever I shall have said to you." Here, then, it is clearly stated that

after Our Lord has died His teaching will
be upheld by the Spirit, but that this indwelling will include also the abiding presence of
Father and Son.

2. Why, then, is it repeated so often that
the Holy Ghost is to be sent into our hearts,
is to be given to us, is to dwell in our midst?
It is for the same reason precisely that we
allocate or attribute certain definite acts to
the Blessed Persons of the Trinity so as the
more easily to discern and appreciate the distinction between Them. In the Creed itself
we attribute creation to God, the Father Al-
mighty, though we know that Son and Spirit,
also with the Father, called the world out of
nothingness. Eternity is often, too, looked
upon as peculiarly of the Father, though
naturally it is common to the Trinity. Note
how frequently in the liturgical prayers of
the Church comes the expression, "O, Eternal Father." So again to the Son we attribute Wisdom and Beauty, turning in our
imagination to Him as the Word of God, the
Figure of His substance, the brightness of
His glory, and to the Holy Spirit we more
often attribute God's love and God's joy.
All these attributions are attempts to make
that high mystery and the Three Persons of
It alive and distinctive to the human spirit.
It is not indeed wholly fancy, but it is the
ever active reason endeavoring, for its own
better understanding of sacred truths, to give

some hint, or find some loophole, whence it shall not be overwhelmed with the greatness of its faith.

3. Consequently, it must be noted that this indwelling of the Spirit of God is not so absolutely and distinctly proper to God, the Holy Ghost, as the Incarnation is proper to God, the Son. There the Son, and He alone, became man. It was His personality alone to which was joined, in a substantial union, human nature. But in this present case there is no such unique connection between the soul and the Spirit of God, but it is rather the Ever Blessed Trinity itself that enters into occupation, and dwells in the heart. Of course that makes the wonder not less, but greater. To think that within the borders of my being is conducted the whole life of the Ever Blessed Three in One; that the Father is for ever knowing Himself in the Son, and that Father and Son are forever loving Themselves in the Spirit; that the power and eternity of the Father, whereby creation was called into being, and by whose fiat the visible world will one day break up and fall to pieces; that the wisdom and beauty of the Son, which catch the soul of man as in the meshes of a net, and drove generations of men to a wandering pilgrimage, at the peril of life, to rescue an empty tomb in the wild fury of a crusade; that the love of the Holy Spirit which completes the

life of God, and was typified in the tongues
of fire and the rush of a great wind at Pentecost; that the power and eternity of the
Father, the wisdom and beauty of the Son,
the love and joy of the Spirit, are for all
time in my heart. O, what reverence for
my human home of God, reverence alike for
soul and body!

This Presence Has Certain Effects

1. It is very clear that so tremendous a presence as this indwelling implies must have tremendous results. If, as I believe, Father, and Son, and Spirit, are always within me by grace, the effect upon my soul should be considerable. To begin with, the very nearness to God which this indwelling secures must make a great difference to my outlook on life. To have within me the Ever Blessed Trinity is more than an honor, it is a responsibility; it is more than responsibility, for it is the greatest grace of all. To my faith, it makes the whole difference in my attitude to the Mother of God that within her womb for those silent months lay the Incarnate Wisdom. If to touch pitch is to ensure defilement, to be so close to God is to catch the infection of His Divinity. Or, again, I may have envied, times out of number, the wonderful grace whereby, upon the breast of his Master, St. John, the Beloved Disciple, could lovingly lay his head, the joy of so close and so familiar an intimacy with the most beautiful sons of men; or I may have pictured the charming scene when on His knees He took the dear children of His country and spoke to them and fondled them

so that in His eyes they could see reflected their own countenances. How life ever after must have been transfigured for them by the memory of that glorious time! Great graces indeed for them all. But what if all life long, by grace, I too can be sure of a union even more splendid, an intimacy more lasting, a friendship surpassing the limits of faith and hope?

2. By grace, then, I receive this indwelling of the Spirit of God, and thereby come into a new and wonderful union with the Ever Blessed Trinity. Now such a union must have its purpose. Our Lord told us that He was going to send to our hearts the Holy Spirit, an embassy from Heaven to earth conducted by a Divine ambassador. The news of the Incarnation, the offer of the Motherhood of God, were made by means of an angel. But here, in my case, to no created official is this wonderful thing confided, only to God Himself. That just shows me the importance of the undertaking. In the political world the interests that turn on a diplomatic mission may be easily guessed to be very great, when the personnel of the staff is found to contain the highest personages in the country. What deep and abiding interests must then be in question when to my soul comes God, the Holy Ghost, sent as the messenger of the Three! I must consequently expect that the results of this in-

dwelling are judged by God to be considerable, and that it is of much moment to me
that, one by one, I should discover them.
The Incarnation brought its train of attend-
ant effects which I have to study: the redemption, the sacraments, the sanctifying of
all immaterial creation by its union through
man with the divinity. This indwelling also
must therefore have its effects, the knowledge
of which must necessarily make a difference
to me in life.

3. By Baptism the beginning comes of
this great grace. As a child, with my senses
hardly at all awake to external life, I had
God in my midst. Do I wonder now at the
charm of early innocence, when a soul sits
silently holding God as its centre? It is not
that there are dim memories of a pre-
existence before birth, but there are always
haunting dreams of a true friendship on
earth. Baptism then begins that early work.
At the moment of conversion, when suddenly
I was drawn into a tender realization of God's
demands and my own heart's hunger, the
indwelling of the Spirit became more con-
sciously operative with its flood of light and
love. Since then the sacraments have poured
out on me fuller measures of God's grace
and that divine Presence therefore should
assume larger proportions in my life. I am
now the dwelling place of God. When, then,
my heart is young, eager, enthusiastic, let

me make Him welcome; nor wait till the only habitation I can offer is in ruins, leaking through an ill-patched roof. A dwelling place for God! How reverently, then, shall I treat and treasure my body and soul, for they must be as fit as I can make them for the great Guest. By reason we learn of Him, by faith we know Him, but by His indwelling we taste the sweetness of His presence.

Forgiveness of Sin

1. To understand this first and great effect of grace I must know what sin is, and to grasp sin in its fullness I must comprehend God. To see the heinousness of what is done against Him I must first realize what He is Himself. I have to go through all my ideas of God, my ideas of His majesty, His power, His tenderness, His justice, His mercy. I have got to realize all that He has done for man before I can take in the meaning of man's actions against God. I have to be conscious of the Incarnation, of the story of that perfect life, the privations of it, the culminating horror of the Passion and Death, then of the Resurrection, the patient teaching of those forty days when He spoke of the Kingdom of God which He was setting up on earth, the Ascension, which did not mean an end, but only the beginning of His work for men on earth. At once there opened the wonderful stream of graces which flow through the sacraments, and which therefore make continuous upon the world till its consummation, His abiding presence, for the tale of the Blessed Sacrament only adds to the wonders of the tenderness and mercy of God. In Heaven, by ever trying

to make intercession for us, on earth, by holding out through the sacraments countless ways of grace, It shows to us something at least of the perfect character of God. Now it is against one so perfect, so tender, so divine, that sin is committed, a wanton, brutal outrage against an almost overfond love. Ingratitude, treachery, disloyalty, united in the basest form.

2. God is just, as well as merciful, so that there had to be an immediate result of sin. Man might see no difference between himself before and after he had sinned; but for all that a great difference was set up. His soul had been on terms of friendship with God, for it had turned irresistibly to Him, as a flower growing in a dark place turns irresistibly to where the hardy daylight makes its way into the gloom. That friendship is at once broken, for sin means that the soul has deliberately turned its back upon God and is facing the other way, and thus it has been able by some fatal power to prevent God's everlasting love having any effect upon it. God cannot hate; but we can stop His love from touching us. At once, then, by grievous sin the soul becomes despoiled of its supernatural goods: sanctifying grace, which is the pledge and expression of God's friendship, naturally is banished; charity, which is nothing else than the love of God, the infused virtues, the gifts, are all taken

away.   Faith only and hope survive, but
emptied of their richness of life.   Externally
no difference, but internally friendship with
God, the right to the eternal heritage, the
merits heretofore stored up—all lost.   Even
God Himself goes out from the midst of the
soul, as the Romans heard the voice crying
from the Temple just before its destruction:
Let us go hence.   Let us go hence.

3. Grace, then, operates to restore all
these lost wonders.   Sin itself is forgiven,
all the ingratitude and disloyalty put one
side; not simply in the sense that God for-
gets them, or chooses not to consider them,
but in the sense that they are completely
wiped away.   It is the parable of the Good
Shepherd where the sheep is brought back
again into the fold, and mixes freely with the
others who have never left the presence of
their Master.   It is the parable of the prodigal son taken back into his father's embrace.
That is what the forgiveness of sin implies.
God is once more back again in the soul.
He had always been there as the Creator
without Whose supporting hand the soul
would be back in its nothingness; but He is
now there again as Father, and Master, and
Friend.   Not the saints only who have been
endowed with a genius for divine things, but
every simple soul that has had its sins forgiven, comes at once into that embrace.   We
are far too apt to look upon forgiveness as

a merely negative thing, a removal, a cleansing, and not enough as a return to something great and good and beautiful, the triumphant entrance into our souls of the Father, the Son, and the Spirit.

JUSTIFICATION

1. There is something in the forgiveness of sin which implies an element of positive good, and this is called justification. It means that the attitude of God towards forgiven sin is believed by the Catholic Church to be no mere neglect or forgetfulness of its evil, but an actual and complete forgiveness. At the time of the Protestant Reformation a long controversy was waged over this very point, in which the Reformers took up the curious position that forgiveness implied nothing more than that God did not impute sin. He covered up the iniquities of the soul with the Blood of His Son, and no longer peered beneath the depths of that sacred and saving sign. The problem has probably hardly any meaning now, since the original doctrinal principles of Protestantism, the ostensible reasons for the sixteenth century revolt, have been abandoned long since as hopeless of defence. In fact all that was really positive in Protestantism has been ruined by its basic negative principle of private judgment. Against such a battering ram Christianity itself is powerless. But that long-forgotten discussion had this much of value, that it brought out in clear perspective the fullness of the Catholic teaching

on the central doctrine of justification and showed its depth and meaning.

2. Briefly, then, it may be stated that it is not simply that God does not impute evil, but that He forgives it. It is as though a rebellion had taken place and its leader had been captured and brought before his offended sovereign. Now the king might do either of two things, if he wished not to punish the culprit. He might simply bid him go off and never appear again, or he might go even further by actually forgiving the rebellion and receiving back into favor the rebel. It is one thing to say that no punishment will be awarded, it is another to say that the crime is forgiven, and that everything is to go on as though nothing had happened. In the first case we might say that the king chose not to impute the sin, in the other that he forgave and justified the sinner. It is just this, then, that the Catholic Church means when she teaches justification as implied in the idea of forgiveness. It is just this, too, that Our Lord meant when He detailed His beautiful parable about the prodigal son. The boy's return home does not mean merely that the father refrains from punishment, but rather that there is a welcome so hearty and so complete that the serious-minded elder brother, coming in from his long labor in the fields, is rather scandalized by its suddenness and its intensity.

Such is indeed God's treatment of the soul. He is so generous, so determined not to be outdone by any sorrow on the part of the sinner, that He overwhelms with the most splendid favors the recently converted soul.

3. But in this connection we must see in justification a process by which the Presence of God is again achieved by man. By sin grace was lost, and with grace went out the Divine Three in One, the temple was desecrated, the veil of the Holy of Holies was utterly rent. Then sin is forgiven and, once more, the Sacred home is occupied by God. Moreover, when God comes to the soul He comes with His full strength of love, and thereby gives a new energy and life to man. We love because of some beauty, goodness, excellence, that we see in others. We love, then, because of what is in them. It is their gifts that cause or ignite our love But God, Who is the only cause Himself, creates excellences by love. We are not loved because we are good; we are good because we are loved, so that this indwelling itself fashions us after God's own heart. "It is the love of God," says St. Thomas (*Summa theologica*, i, 20.2), "that produces and creates goodness in things." The divine presence, then, of God in the soul, effected by sanctifying grace, makes the soul more worthy a temple, more fit a home. God does not come to us because we are fit, but we are fit because God comes to us.

DEIFICATION

1. This very strong expression is used by St. Augustine and many of the Fathers to describe one of the effects of grace. By grace we are deified, i. e., made into gods. Right at the beginning of all the woes of humanity when, in the Garden of Eden, Adam and Eve first were tempted, the lying spirit promised that the reward of disobedience would be that they should become "as gods." The result of sin could hardly be that, so man, made only a little lower than the angels, can at times find himself rebuked by the very beasts. Yet the promise became in the end fulfilled, since the Incarnation really affected that transformation, and God, by becoming human, made man himself divine. St. Peter, in his second epistle (4.1), insinuates the same truth when he describes the great promises of Christ making us "partakers of the Divine Nature." The work, then, of grace is something superhuman and divine. Creation pours into us the divine gift of existence and therefore makes us partakers in the divine being, for existence implies a participatiou in the being of God. The indwelling of the Blessed Trinity, then, does even more, for by it we participate not only in the divine being, but in the divine nature, and fulfill

the prophecy of Our Lord: "Ye are gods." Justification, therefore, is a higher gift than creation, since it does more for us.

2. This divine participation is what is implied in many texts which allude to the sacrament of Baptism, for the purpose of Baptism is just that, to make us children of God. The phrases concerning "new birth" and "being born again" all are intended to convey the same idea, that the soul by means of this sacrament is lifted above its normal existence and lives a new life. This life is lived "with Christ in God," i. e., it is a sort of entrance within the charmed circle of the Trinity, or, more accurately, it is that the Blessed Trinity inhabits our soul and enters into our own small life, which at once therefore takes on a new and higher importance. In it henceforth there can be nothing small or mean. For the same reason Our Lord speaks of it to the Samaritan woman as *"the* gift of God," beside which all His other benefactions fade into nothingness. Again, it is a "fountain of living water," it is a "refreshment," it is "life" itself. Not the stagnant water that remains in a pool in some dark wood, but a stream gushing out from its source, fertilizing the ground on every side, soaking through to all the thirsting roots about it, giving freshness and vitality to the whole district through which it wanders. Life indeed it bears as its great gift;

and so does sanctifying grace carry within it the fertilizing power needed by the soul.

3. The participation in the Divine Nature is therefore no mere metaphor, but is a real fact. The indwelling of God makes the soul like to God. I find myself influenced by the people with whom I live, picking up their expressions, copying their tricks and habits, following out their thoughts, absorbing their principles, growing daily like them. With God at the centre of my life the same effect is produced, and slowly, patiently, almost unconsciously, I find myself infected by His spirit. What He loves becomes my ideal; what He hates, my detestation. But it is even closer than this, no mere concord of wills nor harmony of ideas, a real and true elevation to the life of God. Grace is formally in God, at the back, so to say, of His divine nature, the inner essence of Himself. By receiving it, therefore, I receive something of God, and begin to be able to perform divine actions. I can begin to know God even as I am known, to taste His sweetness, and by His favor to have personal, experimental knowledge of Himself. To act divinely is only possible to those who are made divine. This, then, becomes the formal union with God, its terms, its end, its purpose. Deified, therefore, we become in our essence by grace, in our intelligence by its light, in our will by charity.

ADOPTED SONSHIP

1. Here again we have to realize that the sonship of God is no mere metaphor, no mere name, but a deep and true fact of huge significance: "Behold what manner of charity the Father hath bestowed upon us that we should be called and should be the sons of God!" (1 John 3). We become the sons of God. St. Paul very gladly quotes the saying of a Greek poet that men are the offspring of God, making use of a particular word which necessarily implies that both the begetter and the begotten are of the same nature. A sonship indeed is what Our Lord is Himself incessantly teaching the Apostles to regard as their high privilege, for God is not only His Father, but theirs: "Thus shalt thou pray, Our Father." With the Gospels it is in constant use as the view of God that Christianity came especially to teach. The Epistles are equally insistent on the same view, for St. Paul is perpetually calling to mind the wonderful prerogatives whereby we cry, "Abba: Father." We are spoken of as co-heirs of Christ, as children of God. St. John, St. Peter, and St. James repeat the same message as the evident result of the Incarnation, for by it we learn that God be-

came the Son of Man, and man the son of God.

2. Yet it must also be admitted that this sonship of God, which is the common property of all just souls, and is the result of the indwelling of God in the soul, does not mean that we are so by nature, but only by adoption. Now adoption, as it is practiced by law, implies that the child to be adopted is not already the son, that the new relationship is entered upon entirely at the free choice of the person adopting, that the child becomes the legal heir to the inheritance of the adopting father. It is perfectly evident that all these conditions are fulfilled in the case of God's adoption, for we were certainly no children of His before His adoption of us as sons; strangers we were, estranged indeed by the absence of grace and the high gifts of God. Naturally we were made by Him, but had put ourselves far from Him: "You were as sheep going astray." Then this adoption of us by God was indeed and could only have been at His free choice, through no merits of ours, but solely according to the deliberate action of His own will, for "you have not chosen Me but I have chosen you." "So that it is not of him that willeth nor of him that runneth, but of God that showeth mercy." Finally, the inheritance is indeed ours by right and title of legal inheritance. We are co-heirs with Christ,

and our human nature is lifted up to the level of God; not, of course, that we supplant Him who is by nature the true Son of God, but that we are taken into partnership with Him, and share in Him the wonderful riches of God.

3. Here, then, I may learn the worth and dignity of the Christian name. I am a true son of God, and what else matters upon earth? I have indeed to go about my life with its vocation and all that is entailed in it. I have to work for my living, it may be, or take my place in the family, or lead my own solitary existence. I have to strive to be efficient and effective in the material things of life that fall to my share to be done. But it is this sonship of God that alone makes any matter in the world. In our own time we have heard a very great deal about culture and the ultimate value of the world; but we have seen also to what evil ends so fine a truth may lead men. True culture is not a question of scientific attainments, or mechanical progress, or the discovery of new inventions of destruction, or even of medical and useful sciences; but it is the perfect and complete development of the latent powers of the soul. True culture may indeed make use of sciences and art; perhaps in its most complete sense science and art are needed for the most finished culture of which man is capable; but it is in its very essence the

deepening of his truest desire, the full stretch of his widest flights of fancy, the achievement of his noblest ideals. What nobler ideal, or fancy, or desire, can a man have than to be called and to be the son of God; to know that he has been drawn into the close union of God; to feel within his very essence the presence of God; to have personal experience as the objects of his knowledge and love of the Father, Son, and Spirit?

Heirs of God

1. One of the conditions of adoption is that the newly chosen son should become the legal heir of the new father. Without this legal result or consequence adoption has no meaning. Merely to get a boy to enter a family circle does not imply adoption, for this last has a distinct meaning with a distinct purpose. If, then, we are the heirs of God we are really possessed of a right to His Divine Inheritance. Heaven has been made indeed our home. We speak of it in our hymns as *patria*, which we can translate as the "land of our fathers." We claim it thereby in virtue of our parentage, and our parentage is of God. If, then, He is our Father, not by nature, but by adoption, i. e., by grace, we are none the less His heirs and have some sort of right over His possessions and riches. A father cannot without leave of his adopted son alienate any of the family heirlooms; the adopted son now, by the father's own free act acquires, not indeed dominion over the riches of the home, but, at any rate, an embargo on the father's free exercise of those riches. He could even demand, as against his father, a legal investigation into the due use and investment of

them. His signature is required for every document that relates to them. He has become almost a part-owner of his father's possessions, since he is their legal heir. All this is implied by adoption in its true sense, and therefore it must be intended to apply to us when we are spoken of as God's adopted sons.

2. I can, therefore, truthfully speak of myself as an heir of God. Of course I cannot mean that there is any possible question of "the death of the testator," i. e., of God. That is quite clearly of no significance here. But adoption does give me some sort of claim to the heritage of God. Now the law defines a heritage as that by which a man is made rich. It includes not the riches only, but the source of the riches, so that if I have a claim to God's riches, I have a claim also upon the source of those riches. For the heir is entitled not merely to a legacy, but to the whole of the fortune. I have a right to the whole fortune of God, to the whole universe. At once, as soon as I realize it, the whole of the world is mine. It is the doctrine of the mystics that, misunderstood, led astray the communists of the Middle Ages. These claimed a common ownership of the wealth of all the world, whereas what was intended was that we should look upon the whole world as ours. To me, then, in life, nothing can be strange or distant or apart.

No places can there be where my mind cannot enter and roam at will and feel itself at home; no things can be profane, no people who are not tabernacles of God, no part of life that is not steeped in that living presence. The only possible boundary is the love and the grace of God. There will indeed come evil frontiers beyond which my soul could never dwell. But all else is of God and is therefore my right. All creation is mine; the wonder and beauty of it, life and death, pleasure alike and pain, yield up to me their secrets and disclose the hidden name of God.

3. Here, then, I can find that divine wealth, to inherit which has been the purpose of the adoption by God. Wherever I turn I shall find Him. Whether life has smooth ways or rough, whether she hangs my path with lights or hides me in gloom, I am the heir to all that earth or sea or sky can boast of as their possession. Indeed, these are only the rich things of God, whereas I have a claim upon even more. I have a claim upon the very source of this wealth, that is, upon God Himself, for He is the sole source of all His greatness. I have a right to God Himself. He is mine. He Who holds in the hollow of His hands the fabric of the world, Who with His divine power supports, and with His providence directs, the intricate pattern of the world, has Himself by creation entered deeply into the world; at the heart of every-

thing He lies hid. But even more by grace He comes in a fuller, richer way into the depths of the soul. Here in me are Father, and Son, and Spirit. Dear God, teach me to understand the wonder of this indwelling, to appreciate its worth, to be thankful for its condescension, to reverence its place of choice, to be conscious of its perpetual upholding. By it I am an heir to the fullness of the divine riches. By it I, a creature, possess in His fullness my Creator, Redeemer, Lord.

GUIDANCE IN SPIRITUAL LIFE

1. I have God the Holy Spirit with me. He comes to me in order that I may surrender myself to Him. Of course I cannot merge my personality in His to the extent of having no power of my own, but God has such infinite dominion over the heart of man that He is able to move the will, without in any sense whatever violating its freedom. In the liturgy of the Church there are two or three prayers which speak about God "compelling our rebellious wills." Now for anyone else to "compel my will" would be to destroy it as a will, since, as even Cromwell freely confessed, "the will suffereth no compulsion"; I cannot be made to will against my will. That would be a contradiction, though I can be made to act against my will, for my actions do not necessarily imply that my will is in them. Whereas, then, no one else can move my will without utterly destroying my moral freedom, God can, for He is intimate to the will and moves it, not really as an external but as an internal power. St. Thomas Aquinas repeatedly refers to this and says over and over again the same thing, namely, that God is so intimately united to man, and so powerful, that not only can He

move man to will, but move him to will
freely by affecting, not only the action of
man, but the very mode of the action.

2. Such is man, whether in a state of grace
or not, that his will is in the hands of God,
to be moved by man freely, but not so as to
exclude God's movement. Naturally enough
it is far easier to say this than to explain it.
Indeed the mere statement is all that is
actually binding upon faith, and the particular explanation favored by St. Thomas in
his general acceptance of St. Augustine's
teaching, comes to us largely as of deep and
abiding moment on account of the very clear
reasons given and the great authority of his
name; but in any case there is something
far more special in the guidance of the Holy
Spirit sought for by the soul in its endeavor
to "live godly in Christ Jesus." It has to
yield itself to the promptings of God, be
eager to catch His every whisper, and quick
in its obedience to His every call. For this
to be achieved, the first work is an emptying
out of the soul. Every obstacle has to be
got rid of; any attachment to creatures that
obscures God's light has to be broken through
(though not every attachment to creatures,
since unless I love man whom I see, I cannot
possibly know what love means when applied
to God, nor can I suppose myself to be able
to understand or love God, whom I do not
see). First, then, to cleanse my soul by

leveling and smoothing and clearing its sur-
face and depths.

3. Then I must yield myself into His arms.
I shall not know very often the way He
wishes me to go. It may be only one step
at a time, and then darkness again; or I
may be taken swiftly and surely and openly
along a clear road. That is His business,
not mine, only I must be prepared not to be
able to follow always the meaning of what
He wants of me. It is not necessary at all
that I should know. If I am faithful and
loyal and full of trust, things will gradually
settle themselves, and I shall at least be able
to look back and understand the significance
and purpose of many things that at first
appeared accidental, and even in opposition
to the end I considered God had in view for
me. Thus by looking back I can sometimes
get a shrewd idea of what is to follow; but
often it is only a guess, nothing more than
that. Still, generally, it would seem that
people who surrender themselves to God do
get a sense or a feeling which leads them
right and makes them sure. It is the divine
tenderness stooping to poor muddled humanity and making it transfigured with God's
own glory. The advance, then, whether con-
sciously grasped or not, is in due proportion
to the purity and fidelity of the soul, purity
in its act of cleansing, fidelity in its subjection to the promptings of the Holy Spirit

Gifts of the Holy Spirit

1. To live the spiritual life to its fullness we need the instinctive governances of the Holy Ghost. All day long, and even all through the hours when consciousness is asleep, the Holy Spirit is speaking to us in many ways. He is offering us His heavenly counsel, enlightening our minds to an ever more complete understanding of the deep truths of faith, and generally imparting to us that deep knowledge without which we cannot make advance. Reason and common sense have their own contribution to make in opening our minds and hearts to a proper interpretation of all that is about us and within us; but reason and common sense have themselves also to be supernaturalized, to be illumined by the light of a far higher plane of truth. Hence the need of this divine instinct is patent to anyone who considers the purpose and destiny of the soul. But it is difficult at times to understand and to grasp surely the words of divine wisdom, since by sin's coarseness the refinement of the soul is dulled and rendered but little responsive; or, rather, it is not so much a matter of being responsive to a message as primarily of hearing and understanding it. It seems to

be very obvious that God must be speaking to me almost without ceasing; it is equally obvious that very little of this is noticed.

2. Here, then, am I in the world and needing the governance of God's instinct. Here, too, is this whispered counsel and enlightenment of God, perpetually being made to me. Yet, though made by God, and needed by me, this counsel and enlightenment, I can be certain, must frequently be entirely lost to me. It is as though I lived in a perfectly beautiful country, with stretching landscape about, and beautiful glimpses of hills and woodland, and yet never saw or appreciated the view; as though heavenly music were about me, to which I never paid the slightest attention; as though my best loved friend stood by me and I never lifted my eyes, and so did not know of his presence. Of course it is really a great deal worse than that, for I do not need with an absolute necessity the view, or the music, or the friend; whereas I do most certainly need this divinely offered help, guidance, enlightenment. Hence it is clear that neither my need nor God's instinct suffice. Something else is required by means of which I am able to make use of that instinct, to hear its message, to discover its meaning, to apply its advice to myself; else am I no better than a general who possesses the full plan of his allies, in all its details, but written in a cypher that he cannot read.

3. To produce this reaction or perception is the work of the sevenfold gifts. They are habits infused into the soul, which strengthen its natural powers, and make them responsive to every breath of God and capable of heroic acts of virtue. By the gifts my eyes are made able to see what had else been hidden, my ears quick to catch what had else not been heard; the gifts do not, so to say, supply eye or ear, but make more delicate, refined, sensitive, the eye and ear already there. Their business is to intensify rather than to create powers established in me by grace. Less excellent necessarily than the theological virtues which unite me to God, they are yet more excellent than the other virtues, though, being rooted in charity and thereby linked up among themselves, they are also part of the dowry that charity brings in her train. On this account it is clear that from the moment of Baptism the sevenfold gifts are the possession of the soul, and whosoever holds one holds all; yet by the sacrament of Confirmation it would appear certain that something further is added, some more delicate perception, some livelier sensitiveness; or it may be, as other theologians point out, that by Confirmation they are more steadily fixed in the soul, more fully established, more firmly held. But in any case it is clear what they are to me, habits whereby I am perfected to obey the Holy Spirit of God.

BEATITUDES

1. The possession of the sevenfold gifts results in the performance of certain virtuous acts, for it is perfectly obvious that if I am so blest by the gifts that I find my reason, will, emotions, made increasedly perceptive of divine currents previously lost to me, I can hardly help acting in a new way. I now discover the view about me, and the music, and, consequently, my manner of life must in some ways be different from before. The Vision has come; it cannot simply open my eyes to new things in life without thereby altering that very life itself. Not only shall I find that what seemed to me before to be evil now appears to me to be a blessing; but on that very account what before I tried to avoid, or, having got, tried to be rid of, I shall now accept, perhaps even seek. Similarly, whereas then I was weak, now I am strong; and increase of strength means new activities, new energy put into the old work and finding its way out into works altogether new. My emotions, finally, which perilled and dominated my life, slip now into a subordinate position, and while thereby as actively employed as before, are held under discipline. It is clear, therefore, that the

gifts will not leave me where I was before, but will influence my actions as well as alter my vision.

2. I find, then, that these new habits will develop into new activities. But this means also that I have a new idea as to the means of achieving the full happiness of life. Once upon a time I thought happiness meant comfort, now I see that it means something quite different. My view of happiness has changed. I am therefore obliged to change also my idea as to the means and conditions whereby, and in which, happiness can be found. I had attempted to climb out of my valley over the hills in the west; I now attempt to climb out over the hills to the east. The steps by which once I clambered are useless to me. I must try new ones in the opposite hills. Just that is what Our Lord meant by promulgating His eight Beatitudes. These are just the new blessedness, so to say, which results from finding that happiness now means the knowledge and love of God. Things that previously I fled from, I now seek; things once my bugbear, are now the objects of my delight. Poverty, meekness, mourning, the hunger and thirst after justice, cleanness of heart, the making of peace, mercy, the suffering of persecution for justice's sake, are now found to be the steps to be passed over, the conditions to be secured before happiness can be finally secured.

3. These things, then, are beatitudes to me. They are acts which I finally achieve by means of the new enlightenment gained through the gifts of God. Actively I am merciful and meek and clean of heart. I perform these actions, and they are the result of visions seen, and counsels heard, through the new sensitiveness to the divine instinctive guidance that of old passed me by without finding in my heart any response. To be forever pursuing now peace and sorrow, and, at whatever cost, justice, is an energizing state of life which is due entirely to the new perception of the value of these things, so that we are right in asserting that the beatitudes are nothing else than certain actions, praised by Our Lord and practiced by us as a result of the establishment in our souls of seven definite habits. But not only are they actions, they produce as an effect joy in the heart; for which reason it is that we call them beatitudes. They show me what is truly blessed and thereby give me, even here on earth, a foretaste of the bliss of final happiness.

THE FRUITS OF THE SPIRIT

1. Besides the beatitudes there are other acts that follow from the gifts when properly used by the soul. The beatitudes are means which, under the light infused by God, are valued at their true worth as leading finally to happiness in its more complete sense. But when these are thus put into practice, for the soul understands the new meaning life gathers, they do not end the wonders of the action of grace. As a boy I met life and found it full of interest and dawning with the glories of success. The world in its aspect of nature had such manifest beauties that these quickly entranced and thrilled the soul. The sun and grass and flowers and woods and waters, make no secret of their kinship with their creator; Francis Thompson found them "garrulous of God," so garrulous in our youth that we see that life is full of very good things. Then comes the reaction (to many even before full manhood), when life is found to be full of illusion. Life is now judged a melancholy business, apt to fail you just when the need of it is most discovered, hard to be certain of; it is the age of romantic melancholy when most people put into verse their

sorrow at the disappointment to be found in
all things of beauty. Every tree and flower
and "dear gazelle" is no sooner loved than
it is lost through death or misunderstanding.

2. Then, finally, the balance is set right.
The two phases pass. They are both true
only as half truths. There is no denying
that life is good and beautiful and thrilling.
The boy's vision is correct. Yet it is equally
true to say that there is sorrow and suffering and death and disappointment in all human things. But a new phase, blessedly a
last phase, dawns upon the soul. Sorrow
and pain are real, but the old happiness of
boyhood is made to fit in and triumph over
them by the sudden realization that strength
is the lesson to be learned. Sorrow comes
that discipline may be born in the soul, self-
restraint, humility. Life is hard, but its
very hardness is no evil, but our means of
achieving good. That is the very atmos-
phere of the beatitudes, the message they
bring, the teaching they imparted from the
Sermon on the Mount. Poverty, cleanness
of heart, mercy, meekness, are all things
difficult to acquire; but they give a real, true
blessedness to the soul that will see their
value. Life is no longer a disappointment,
but the training ground of all good.

3. Finally, there follow other acts, too
many to number, though there are twelve
usually given, which result from gifts and

beatitudes. These are called the fruits of the Holy Ghost, for they represent in that metaphorical sense the ultimate result of the gifts. They are the last and sweetest consequences of the sevenfold habits infused by the Spirit. Indeed, just as trees are grown in an orchard because of their fruits, and, therefore, just as it can be said that the fruit is, from the gardener's point of view, the purpose for which the tree is cultivated (for of the fruitless fig Our Lord asked why it cumbered the ground), so these fruits of the Holy Ghost (charity, joy, peace, patience, benignity, goodness, longanimity, mildness, faith, modesty, continency, chastity —Gal. 5.22) can be looked upon as the very purpose for which the gifts were given, that I might, by seeing a new blessedness in life's very troubles, begin to find joy and peace and patience and faith, where else I had found only sorrow. Endlessly could the list of these be extended, for St. Paul has chosen only a very few; but these that he names are what a man delights in when he has received the gifts, and has understood and valued the beatitudes. Sweetness is what they add to virtue, ease, comfort. I not only hunger and thirst after justice, but enjoy the very pain of the pursuit.

Knowledge

1. This gift of God illumines and perfects the intelligence. The purpose of the gifts, it has been already explained, is to make the soul more alive to, and more appreciative of, the whispered instinct of God; not to create new faculties, but to increase the power of those already existing. My mind, then, has to be supernaturalized and refined to that pitch of perception which will enable it to grasp and to understand God's message. Now the mind itself works upon a great variety of subjects. It has whole worlds to conquer, planes of thought which are very clearly distinguishable; yet in its every activity it needs this divine refinement, so that in all four gifts are allotted to perform this complete enlightenment of the mind. Knowledge overcomes ignorance and is concerned with the facts, visible and sense-perceived, in creation; for by the council of the Vatican it is laid down as part of the deposit of faith that human reason can prove the existence of God altogether apart from the supernatural motives which grace supplies. The visible world is held to contain ample proofs which in themselves are adequate logically to convince human understanding of the existence of God. Individual reason may fail to sat-

isfy itself. People may declare truthfully
that they are not convinced; the Church in-
sists only that it can be done.

2. Knowledge, however, in this sense is a
gift of God whereby we discover Him in His
own creation and in the works of man. It
is here no mere task set to reason for detect-
ing the Creator in His handiwork, but an
actual vision by which the soul is supernaturalized and sees Him patently everywhere. The beauteous face of nature is
merely seen as a veil, hiding a beauty more
sublime. Things of dread as well as things
of loveliness come into the scheme, things
trivial and things tremendous, things majes-
tic and things homely, all that God has made.
Even man's work, who is himself only one of
the greater masterpieces of the Great Artificer, is affected by this new light with which
the world is flooded. The delicate pieces of
machinery constructed by human ingenuity,
that gain in wonder and in power, are themselves still God's work at one remove; they
are the fruits of a mind that He has constructed, and they do not exhaust the capacity of that mind. They reveal hidden
potentialities as well as express actual
achievements. Weapons of destruction, with
all the horror they rightly inspire, are yet
witnesses again to that parent-intelligence
whence was begotten man himself. All this,
of course, as soon as considered, is admitted

by every believer in God, but the gift of knowledge makes it realized and seen steadfastly.

3. Life, then, of itself is full of illusion. That is the cry, desolating and pitiful, which arises from the higher followers of every religious faith. Man is bound to the wheel, his mind is compassed with infirmity, he is born into ignorance. Desire tumultuously hustles all his days. He needs, therefore, some light whereby he may find the true inner meaning of all with which he comes in contact. Here, then, in the gift of Knowledge is such a true vision, understanding, vouchsafed him of the visible things of creation. He will realize as much, perhaps, even more than before the attraction of beauty, only it will be no snare, but a beckoning light. He will find in it now no illusion, but the perfect image of a greater beauty. The charm of the world about him will become greater, the wonders of nature, the intricate pattern of mechanical appliances, the fury of storms, the tumult of the wind, the terrific force of pestilence, the psychological facts of man's mind, the construction of his frame, the grouping of his social instincts, all now will be alive with God, shot through with the divine splendor, elevated to His order of life, eloquent of His name—a deepening knowledge of God achieved through a knowledge of His creatures.

UNDERSTANDING

1. There is another gift required to perfect the intelligence when it is engaged upon the principles of truth. The mind was created by God to exercise itself upon truth, primarily, the Supreme Truth; secondarily, all truths which by their essence must themselves be radiations from the Supreme Truth. These truths are of endless variety, both in their relationship to each other and in the particular line in which they operate. They are the truths of arts and science, the intricate yet unchanging laws that govern the growth and development of matter, the complicated processes whereby organic beings build up their tissues and multiply themselves by means of the cell principle. There are again the curious laws, as they are called, that effect gravitation, that have to be counted upon in the science of architecture, and in all the various kindred crafts of man. There are principles, too, that underlie the whole series of the arts, principles of truth and life and beauty. Upon these the mind must feed, and in them all the mind must be able to trace the character and being of God. But there are also far higher truths which are taught only by revelation, safeguarded by authority, grouped under the title of faith. These truths are higher than the

others, since they directly concern a higher being, i. e., God. All truths are truths about God, but the truths of faith concern themselves immediately with the being, life, and actions of God. Understanding, therefore, is the gift perfecting the mind for these.

2. It might seem, perhaps, that the light of faith is itself sufficient, and that no further gift were needed, since it is the very purpose of faith to make us accept this revelation of God, enlightening and strengthening the intelligence till under the dominion of the will it says: I believe. It is true that faith suffices for this, but we require something more than faith, or at least if we do not absolutely require more, we shall progress more rapidly and further when we are not only able to believe but to understand. In every article of faith there is always something which is mysterious or hidden, some obscurity due not to the entanglement of facts, but to the weakness of the human mind. Of course this must to some extent always exist, for man can never hope to comprehend God till by the beatific vision he sees Him face to face; but a good deal of the obscurity can be lifted by the mere operation of the mind under the light of God, not arising purely from study, but from the depth of love enkindled by God. It is a commonplace in the lives of the saints that without instruction they do yet manage to learn the deep mysteries of God; the same

rue **of many simple souls whom we meet**
n time to time in the world. They not
; believe, **but penetrate the truths of faith.**
. Here, then, I have ready to hand a most
'ul gift of God. I desire not only to be-
:, but to absorb and to penetrate the mys-
:s of God. I want to taste to the full
meaning of life as a whole, to develop
·y power that lies in me, to make the
.hs of revelation blossom out ever more
y, till their hidden and mystical signifi-
:e becomes gradually more clear. The
:s of Holy Scripture are full of instruc-
, but they will not yield up their secrets
to a soul attuned by God. That can be
·ted by the gift of understanding. I
l find by its means that these treasures
inexhaustible, that from mere abstract
hing the sayings of the Master and His
)stles become full of practical meaning,
all life about me takes on a new and
er significance. History and social life
their doors to whoever has this blessed
, and it becomes clearly seen that their
er and builder is God. The dullness of
s who will not believe, or only believe
then stop short, becomes painful to note
bothersome to put up with, but this is
price one has to pay for so fine a vision.
this, then, we peer into the depths of
h, and find them gradually and steadily
ving more and more clear and penetrable.

Wisdom

1. All writers on the gifts of the Holy Ghost place wisdom as the highest gift of all. It takes this high position partly because its work is done in the intelligence, which is man's highest power, and partly because it is that highest power occupied to its highest capacity. Like knowledge and understanding, its business is to make us see God everywhere, in the material and spiritual creation of God, in the concrete facts of existence, and in the revealed truths of faith. It produces in a soul a sense of complete certainty and hope. Hence it is sometimes described as neighbor to hope; indeed, its finest side is often just that determined and resolute conviction with which the soul rises superior to every possible disaster, and is prepared to brave every contingency in its sureness of God's final power and the efficacy of His will. It comes closer, therefore, to God Himself than do either understanding or knowledge. These do, indeed, enable the soul to be continuously conscious of the divine presence, of God immanent as well as transcendent, God in the heart of the world as well as wholly above the world, and they affect this consciousness by enabling the soul to see Him everywhere   They lift the veil. They show

His footprints. They trace everywhere the
marks of His power, wisdom, love. But it
is noticeable that they lead to God from the
world. I see a flower, and by the gift of
knowledge I am immediately aware of the
author of its loveliness; by understanding I
perceive with clearness the wonder of God's
working in the world. By them I lift my
eyes from earth to Heaven, by wisdom I look
from Heaven to see the earth.

2. Wisdom, therefore, implies an understanding of the world through God, whereas
knowledge and understanding suppose a perception of God through the world. Wisdom
takes its stand upon causes, the other two
on effects. They work from creatures to
Creator; wisdom looks upon all the world
through the eyes of God. Consequently the
effect of wisdom is that the soul sees life as
a whole. Matter and truth are to it no longer
separate planes of thought, but one. There
is at once no distinction between them in the
eyes of God, for both are manifestations of
Himself and creatures of His making. Hence
the soul that is dowered with wisdom climbs
up to God's own height, and looking down
upon the world sees it "very good," noticing
how part fits in with part, and how truths
of faith, and truths of science and sunset,
and flower and Hell, are linked one with another to form the pattern of God's design.
Each has its place in the divine economy of

God's plan, each is equally of God, equally
sharing in His purposes, though some more
than others able to express God better. The
effect, then, is largely that the whole of life
is co-ordinated, and equality, fraternity, lib-
erty, become not the motto of a revolution,
but of the ordered government of God.

3. The opposite to this gift is folly, for
a man who fails in wisdom loses all true judgment of the values of human life. He is perpetually exchanging the more for the less
valuable, bestowing huge gifts in just bar-
ter, as he imagines, for what is merely showy
and trivial. Not by causes, but by effect
does he consider life and its activities. The
wise man, then, estimates everything by its
highest cause. He compares and discovers,
gleans the reason of God's providence, its
purpose, its fitness. First principles are his
guide, not the ready and practical proverbs
that display the wit and worldly wisdom of
the lesser man. Eternity becomes of larger
moment than time, since time is merely for
eternity. God's law is more convincing than
man's, for man's enactments are not laws at
all when they come in conflict with divine
commands. Faith is so deeply in him that
he judges between propositions, and discovers truth against heresy. He has climbed
to the heights of God and sees all the world
at his feet, and knows it as God knows it,
the world and its Lord and the glory of it.

Counsel

1. The fourth gift that perfects the intelligence acts rather as a moderating than as a stimulating influence The soul is often impetuous in its decisions, moved by human feelings and passions, urged by desire, love, hatred, prejudice. Quickly stirred to action, it dashes into its course without any real attention to, or understanding of, its better wisdom. Frequently in life my lament has to be that I acted on the impulse of the moment. There is so much that I am sorry for, not merely because now I see what has actually resulted, but because even then I had quite sufficient reason to let me be certain what would result. I was blind, not because my eyes could not have seen, but because I gave them no leave to see. I would not carefully gaze at the difficulties, not puzzle out in patience what would most likely be the result. Even my highest powers are often my most perilous guides, since, moved by generosity, I engaged myself to do what I have no right to perform, and find that I have in the end been generous not only of what is my own, but sometimes of what belongs to another, not as though I deliberately gave away what belonged to another, but just because I had no deliberation at all. I

need, then, the Holy Spirit of God to endow me with the gift of counsel which corresponds to prudence.

2. Now prudence, which counsel helps and protects, is eminently a practical gift of God, not so high as wisdom, not so wonderful in the beauty of its vision as knowledge or understanding, yet for all a most important and homely need. The other intellectual gifts of the Spirit are more abstract. They give us just the whisper of God that enables us to see the large ways of God in the world. They give, in consequence, the great principles that are to govern us in life. Hence their importance is very great. We do so seriously need to know by what principles we are to measure life's activities, on what basis to build up the fabric of our souls, to be sure that God's laws are very clearly and definitely made manifest to us. But, after all, that is only one-half of the difficulty, for even after I know the principles of action, I have still the trouble, in some ways more full of possibilities of mistake, of applying them to concrete experience. I know that sacrifice is the law of life, I know that meekness overindulged may be cowardice, I know that I may sin by not having anger; that is all evident, a series of platitudes. But here, and now, have I come to the limit of meekness? Must I manifest my angry protests? Am I obliged to attend to my own needs and

renounce the idea of sacrifice? There daily are questions that puzzle, torture, bruise me with scruples.

3. Just here, then, I have intense need for this practical gift of God in order with nicety and precision to apply principles to concrete cases; often I am precipitate or perhaps dilatory. I am in a hurry or cannot make up my mind—shall I answer those who attack me, or shall I be silent? Our Lord was silent and made answer by turns. Counsel, then, is my need from God, the instinct whereby a practical judgment is quickly and safely made. All the more have I a tremeudous need for this if my life is full of activity, if pressure of work, or social life, or the demands of good and useful projects, or the general tendency of my family surroundings, make my day crowded and absorbed, for the very combined and concentrated essence of life will need some exceedingly moderate influence to produce any sense of balance or proportion in my judgment. The people about me I notice to become more and more irritable, mere creatures of impulse. I feel some such malign influence invading the peaceful sanctuary of my soul, disturbing its even outlook on things, driving out my serene calm. I must anchor on to this gift of God, become prudent, detached, filling the mind with the counsel of the Holy Spirit.

FORTITUDE

1. After the intelligence comes the will which also, because of the very large part it plays in all human action, needs to be perfected by a gift of the Spirit. It is necessary to repeat that the Holy Spirit does not by His gifts bestow on the soul new powers and new faculties, but develops, refines, perfeets faculties already there. It is not the creation of new eyes to see new visions, but the strengthening of the eyes of the soul so as to see more clearly and with a longer sight. The will, then, has also to be strengthened, for it is the will that lies at the very heart of all heroism. Merely to have a glimpse of greatness is but part of a hero's need. No doubt it is a larger part, for very many of us never by instinct at all touch on the borders of greatness, we do not see or understand how in our little lives we can be great, we have not the imagination lit up by God, no vision; yet "when the vision fails, the people shall perish." But even when that sudden showing does by God's mercy come to us, we still fall far short of it. It is too high, too ideal, too far removed from weak human nature to seem possible to us. That is to say, our will has failed us. We are faced by

some huge obstacle, or even by a persistent refusal to budge on behalf of some one (ourselves or another) to go forward and to do; we struggle, fail, lose heart, surrender, cease our efforts. What do we want? Fortitude, that "persistive constancy" that to Shakespeare was the greatest quality of human wills.

2. How is this achieved? By appreciating the nearness of God to us. The gifts make us responsive to God with an ease and instantaneousness that operates smoothly and without friction. That is God's doing, not ours. He gives us this wonderful power of being able to register at once every passing inspiration. The gifts that refine the intelligence allow it to perceive sights which else were hidden. The gift that refines the will must do this by some kindred action. Now the difficulties that beset the will must necessarily be difficulties for whose overcoming strength is needed. Therefore the will must be refined by being made strong. How can it be made strong by the Holy Spirit? What exactly happens to its mechanism to secure for it the power of endurance? The easiest way of understanding how this effect is brought about is to suppose that the soul by its refinement, by that delicacy whereby it responds instantly to a divine impression, is quickly aware of God's nearness to it. It perceives how close it is to the Spirit of God, and the sense of this nearness makes

it better able to hold on to its duty. In the old style of warfare we often read of wives and mothers coming to the field of battle that their presence might awake their men to the topmost pitch of courage. Even in the modern methods of fighting, the moral effect of the presence of the emperor or king is considered to have an effect upon the troops. Of course here it is more homely, since the familiar presence of the Holy Spirit strengthens and inspires by love, trust, sympathy.

3. For this reason the name Comforter was given to the Holy Spirit, in its original sense of strengthening, becoming the fort of the soul; and the result is that the recipient is able to hold on or, in our modern slang, to "carry on." By nature so many of us are prone to seek our own comforts at the expense of what we know to be the higher side of us. Human respect makes us again cowardly, or the sheer monotony of perseverance dulls and wearies the soul. We get so depressed with the strain of making efforts that we are very much inclined to let the spiritual side of life go under, or at least be rendered as little heroic as possible, for it is real heroism even just to "go on." The "silent pressure" of temptations, when their passion and fury have died down, is a constant worry, an unconscious weight on the mind, like the thought of war that lies heavily at the back of the consciousness of those

whose external lives seem empty of war-re-
minders. We want to be courageous and
fearless, to *undergo*. Then we must hold
fast to God's nearness to us, and feel the
virtue going out from Him to us, though He
does but touch the hem of our garments by
His indwelling.

PIETY

1. Besides our intelligence and will we have other faculties that go by a diversity of names; sometimes they are called the emotions, sometimes the passions, sometimes they are alluded to as the sentimental side of our nature; but by whatever name we may happen to call them, it is clear that they represent just those movements of our being which are not really rational in themselves, though they can be controlled by the reason. It is simplest to divide them into two classes and to realize that they lie just on the borderline between spirit and matter, partly of soul, partly of body. These two classes are arranged according as the emotion attracts or repels man. The repelled emotions are fear, anger, hatred, etc.; the attracted are love, desire, joy, etc. This gift of piety enables even the emotions to be made responsive to God. It is always the notion of some perfect instrument to be made harmonious that perhaps most clearly shows us the work of the Holy Spirit in the gifts of God, some perfect instrument, which needs to be so nicely attuned that its every string shall give out a distinct note, and shall require the least movement from the fingers of God's right hand to

make its immediate response. Here, then, we have first to record the fact that the purpose of this gift is to make the emotions or passions so refined, so perfectly strung, that at once the slightest pressure of the Divine instinct moves them to turn their love, desire, joy, towards God, finding in Him the satisfaction of their inmost heart.

2. Piety, in its Latin significance (and here in theology, of course, we get almost all our terms through the Latin tongue), means the filial spirit of reverence towards parents. Virgil gives to the hero of his Roman epic the repeated title of *pius*, because he wishes always to emphasize Æneas' devotion to his aged father. Hence it is clear that what is primarily intended here is that we should be quickly conscious of the Fatherhood of God. The mediæval mystics, especially our homely English ones like Richard Rolle of Hampole, and Mother Julianna of Norwich, curiously enough were fond of talking about the Motherhood of God in order to bring out the protective and devoted side of God's care for us; of course God surpasses both a mother's and father's love in His ineffable love for us. But then it is just that sweetness of soul in its attitude towards God, that this gift produces in me a readiness to perceive His love in every turn of fortune, and to discover His gracious pity in His treatment of my life. It requires a divine indwelling of the

Spirit of God to effect this in my soul, for though I may be by nature easily moved to affection, prompt to see and profit by every opening for friendship, yet I must, no less, have a difficulty in turning this into my religious life without God's movement in my soul.

3. Perhaps the most unmistakable result of this is in the general difference between Catholic and non-Catholic nations, in their ideas of religion. Even if one takes a non-Catholic nation at its best and a Catholic nation at its worst, the gulf between them is enormous, for at its lowest the religion of the Catholic nation will be attractive at least with its joy, and the non-Catholic repellent with its gloom. There is a certain hardness about all other denominations of Christianity, a certain restrained attitude of awe towards God, which though admirable in itself, is perfectly hateful when it is made the dominant note in religion. Better joyous superstition than gloomy correctness of worship; better, far better, to find happy childrn who have little respect, and much comradeship, towards their parents, than neat and quiet children who are in silent awe of their parents. It is, then, to develop this side of religion that the gift of piety is given. The result then is a sweetness, a gracefulness, a natural lovingness towards God and all holy persons and things, as opposed to a

gloomy, respectable, awkward, self-conscious hardness towards our Father in Heaven. Clever, trained people have most to be on their guard, for the intellectual activities of the soul are apt to crowd out the gentler, simpler side of character.

FEAR

1. Catholics as a whole, then, we claim to be not in awe of God, but holding themselves to Him rather by love than fear; yet for all that there must come into our religion a notion also of fear, else God will be made of little account, dwarfed by His hero-followers, the saints. It is possible that familiarity with God may breed something which seems very like contempt. The majesty of God has got to be considered just as much as His love, for either without the other would really give a false idea of Him. Just as there are people who would give up all belief in Hell, because they prefer to concentrate upon His mercy, and, as a result, have no real love of God as He is in Himself, so there are people also who do not sufficiently remember the respect due to His awfulness, people who think of Him as a Redeemer, which indeed He is, but not as a Judge, which is equally His prerogative. Hence this side of our character is also to be made perfect by the indwelling of the Spirit of God, our fear, anger, hate, have got to be sanctified by finding a true object for their due exercise. No single talent must be wrapped away in uselessness; I must fear God, be angry with, and

hate sin. Fear, then, as well as piety is a gift of the Spirit.

2. The chief way in which the absence of this gift of fear manifests itself is in the careless and slipshod way we perform our duties. We are sure to believe in God's justice and majesty; but we are not so sure to act up to our belief. Accuracy in devotion, in prayer, in life, is the result of a filial fear of God, and if I have to confess a very chaotic and uncertain procedure in my spiritual duties, then I can tell quite easily which gift I most need to make use of. What are my times for prayer like? Are they as regularly kept to as my circumstances permit? How about my subject for meditation, how about my following of the Mass, my watchfulness in prayer, my days for confession and communion? Again, my duties at home, in my profession, in the work I have undertaken? Are they on the whole punctually performed, accurately, with regard to details? That is where my fear for God should come in, for fear here is part of love and love is enormously devoted to little things, indeed finds that where it is concerned there are no little things, but time and place and manner and thoroughness have all got faithfully to be noted and carried out. Here, then, is where I shall find I need a reverential fear of God.

3. Yes, of course, pride and laziness will protest all the while, by urging that all this is

a great deal of fuss about nothing, that God is our Father, that He perfectly understands, that we should not worry ourselves too much over trifles. Now pride and laziness often speak true things, or rather half-truths. It is true that God is my Father and understands; but it is equally true that I am His child and that love demands my thoroughness. Horror of sin, devotion to the sacrament of confession, the Scripture saying about a severe judgment for every idle word, all these things have got to be taken into account as well as the first set of principles. Piety needs fear for its perfect performance. The boy at first may have to be scolded into obedience to his mother. He does not at first realize, and is punished; but watch him when he is a grown man, no longer in subjection or under obedience; see how charmingly he cares for her by anticipating her wishes, how much he is at her beck and call, proudly foreseeing for her, protecting, caring. That is love, no doubt, but a love of reverence. They are comrades in a sense, but she is always his mother to him, some one to be idolized, reverenced, yes, and, really, feared, in the fullest sense of love.

GRACE

I. The indwelling, then, of the Holy Spirit
is a true and magnificent phrase. It means
that we become living Temples of God. Elsewhere indeed He is in tree, flower, sky, earth,
water; up in the Heavens, down to the depths
of the lower places, in the cleft wood and
lifted stone, in the heart of all creation by
the very fact of its creation. Yet the higher
a thing is in the scale of being the more nearly
is it after God's image and likeness, so that
man by his sheer intelligence is more representative of God, as the highest masterpiece
is more representative of the author of it.
Yet over and above this intelligent life of
man is another life in him, which secures
God's presence within him in some nobler
fashion, for it is noticeable that Scripture
repeatedly speaks of God's dwelling in His
saints, and not dwelling in sinners. Now He
is even in sinners by the title of their Creator,
so that *dwelling* must be a deliberate phrase
chosen by the Inspired author of Scripture
to represent some presence above the mere
general presence of God everywhere. Consequently we are driven to the conclusion
that the saints, in virtue of their sainthood,
become dwelling places of God, temples, spe-

cial places set apart, where in a more perfect way, with richer expression and more true representation, God is. Sanctity, therefore, constitutes something wholly supernatural, attracting God's indwelling, or rather resulting from this indwelling of God.

2. Now sanctity itself cannot mean that one man is able to make himself so alluring to God that he draws God to himself, for in that case God's action of indwelling would be motived by a creature, and God would have found some finite reason for His act. This cannot be, since the only sufficient motive for God can be God Himself. "He hath done all things on account of Himself," say the Scriptures. We can be sure, therefore, that the indwelling of the spirit is the cause and not the effect of the goodness that is in man, for the Saints are not born, but made by God. Hence we understand what is meant by saying that the justice of the Saints, their justification, is effected by grace, i. e., by God's free gift. It is not from them, but from Him: "Not to us, O Lord, not to us, but to Thy name give Glory." *Grace*, therefore, is the name given to that divine habit whereby the soul is made one with Him. It is clear, then, also, why in the catechism grace is called the supernatural life of the soul, and why mortal sin is called the death of the soul, since it kills the soul by depriving it of sanctifying grace.

3. This leads us to the last notion of grace, that it is in the supernatural order what the soul is in the natural order. My soul is everywhere in my body and gives evidence of its presence by the life there manifest; cut off a portion of the body, amputate a limb. It dies. The soul is no longer in it. So does grace work. It is right in the very essence of the soul, at the heart of it, and works through into all the faculties and powers by means of the virtues. It is the life of the whole assemblage of these habits of goodness. As soon as it is withdrawn, then at once charity goes, for we are out of friendship with God, and charity is nothing other than the love of God. Hope still and faith in some form remain, but without any inner life or energy to quicken them. All else is a crumbled ruin, without shape or life, a sight to fill those that can see it with horror and disgust. With grace the soul is once more thronged with vital activities, for grace is life. Grace it is that gives the same charm to the soul as life gives to the body; it imparts a freshness, an alertness, an elasticity, a spontaneous movement, a fragrance, a youth. By grace we are children in God's eyes, with the delicate coloring and sweetness of a child; without it we are old, worn, dead, not only useless to ourselves, but a pollution to others. Need one wonder if all life is different to the soul in sin? Religion, God,

Heaven, Mass, prayers, have lost all attraction and are full of drudgery. Outwardly
we feel the same; but our attraction to these
higher gifts has gone, a prodigal as yet content with the husks of life's fruitage, relish-
ing only the food of swine, without grace,
spiritually dead.